P9-CJS-733

TOKEN CHICK

A Woman's Guide to Golfing with the Boys

CHERYL LADD

WITH BOB HELLMAN

A Roundtable Press Book

miramax books

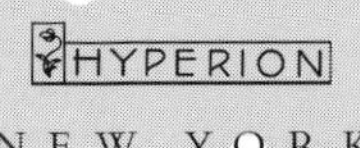

NEW YORK

Printed in the United States of America.

For information address:
Hyperion
77 West 66th Street
New York, New York
10023-6298.

ISBN 1-4013-5222-7

first edition

10 9 8 7 6 5 4 3 2 1

Photos on pages 5 (bottom right), 7, 43-45, 62 (bottom), 75, 112-113, 126-133, 207– 222: Bob Hellman

Photo on page 6: Lee Salem

Photos on pages 8, 26, 46, 64, 76, 90, 98, 114, 128, 134, 140, 194, 202, 212, 248, 266, 280, 288: ©Corbis

Photo on page 24: Mark Glassman/Palm Desert

Photo on page 25: www.lightworksphotography.com

Photo on page 142: Paul Lester

Photo on page 145: IP (Insta-Plak, Inc.)

All other photos: Cheryl Ladd

A Roundtable Press Book

Directors: Julie Merberg and Marsha Melnick

Executive Editor: Patty Brown

Editor: John Glenn

Design: Georgia Rucker

Acknowledgments

A million thanks to my husband Brian Russell; Jay Schwartz, who encouraged me to write this book; Dan Strone, who convinced me that there was a market for it; Bob Hellman for keeping me in stitches; Carmé Tenuta for her artistry; and Teresa Gutierrez for the great clothes. My pro-am partners for their patience and for teaching me the hacker's motto: humor and humility. Beth Daniel for all her help and a very special thank you to all the LPGA, PGA, and Champions Tour players for including me and encouraging me. And most of all a big thank you to Miramax Books for their *fore*sight.

TABLE OF CONTENTS

INTRODUCTION

Hello. My name is Cheryl, and I'm a golfaholic.

I'd like to thank you for getting my book. It's been a long time in the making. Over twenty years. Not that I've been writing it for twenty years, but it's taken me that long to get here. Where am I? Scrambling for a par, putting for a skin, remembering my swing thoughts, and looking forward to the nineteenth hole. If you're nodding your head in agreement, it's nice to meet you. If you're a little confused by my terminology, don't worry, you won't be for long.

To get things started, let me tell you what it means to be a token chick. If Webster's dictionary had a definition for the term token chick, it might read, "One lone female representing her species against a large cavalry of sometimes chauvinistic men, thus making her the token chick." (Well, maybe that would be in Webster's female dictionary.) A token chick can be anything from being the only woman in an office filled with men, growing up with three older brothers, or finding golf tees in the bottom of your evening bag. It's an attitude. It's a metaphor.

If a picture is worth a thousand words, then this one needs only two: "token chick." It's from the first AFI Celebrity Golf

Classic at Riviera Country Club in Los Angeles. What a lineup of men: Michael Keaton, Sylvester Stallone, James Woods, Jack Lemmon, Greg Kinnear, Scott Wolf, Robert Wagner, Sidney Poitier, Samuel L. Jackson, Arnold Schwarzenegger, and Andy Garcia. It's a great guest list for the ultimate bachelorette party!

Here I am again, six years later and two things are for sure. I'm still the token chick, and my buddy Robert Wagner stands next to me during every group shot!

I've put together some of my favorite stories, pictures, and tips from the golfing adventures I've been fortunate enough to experience.

I hope you enjoy reading this book as much as I've enjoyed living it. I thank my husband, Brian, for introducing me to the game. He gave me the greatest gift in the world—the game of golf. Now I only have one more thing to say:

Let's tee it up!

Reason number one why I'm the token chick

HOW I GOT HOOKED

If you play golf, you probably remember how you got hooked. Maybe your dad took you to the driving range when you were young, or you got interested as an adult. For me it was almost accidental. It certainly wasn't something that I had even been thinking about pursuing. Golf came completely out of left field. Actually, it came from the living room. I was in my kitchen when my husband Brian walked in. Now I know many books start out with, "It was a bright, sunny day . . . ," but it was. Don't forget, I live in Southern California. It's usually a bright, sunny day. This particular day was even brighter and sunnier than normal—less smog than usual.

Brian walked into the kitchen on a mission. A mission any man would be on if he'd been born in a town called Falkirk that sits smack dab in the center of Scotland. A golf mission. Growing up in Scotland, Brian's dad introduced him to the game. It's practically a right of passage where he's from. Brian enjoyed playing, but as with many people, life happens and golf takes a back seat. A few decades would pass before Brian realized that golf should not take a back seat anymore. It should sit up front, with both of us. That's when he walked into the kitchen with the news. He wanted, correction, *needed* to play golf.

If I ever do a movie about a wife whose husband gets her hooked on golf, I already have the first page of my script.

KITCHEN – MORNING

(BRIAN ENTERS ON A MISSION)

BRIAN

Let's play golf.

CHERYL

Excuse me?

BRIAN

Golf. I want to play golf. I need to play golf.

CHERYL

Honey, is there something you're not telling me?

BRIAN

I'm Scottish.

CHERYL

I know. It's one of your best features.

BRIAN

Well, having been born and bred in Scotland,
I need to be doing more things that are Scottish.
We need to be more Scottish . . . as a couple.

CHERYL

Fine, but I'm not eating haggis.

BRIAN

I am talking about golf. We should be playing golf. It's in my genes. It's my heritage, my history. Scots invented golf! I may have a God-given gift for the game, and I've got to find out. Today.

CHERYL

Alrighty then! Men . . .

If you're married, it's sometimes just easier to agree with your partner than not. Besides, what if he was right? What if the good Lord actually did bestow him with golf superpowers; after all, he is Scottish! I was definitely intrigued. I put on a tennis shirt (since it was the closest thing in my wardrobe to golf attire), and off we went.

We got in the car and headed to the only golf course we knew, Rancho Park Golf Club. It's a municipal course that's been in Los Angeles for over fifty years. It's a nice mixture of old meets new. A massive clubhouse, a course of old-fashioned design, and a modern two-tiered driving range. In its heyday, Rancho Park was a prime stop on the professional golf tour. If you visit Los Angeles, make sure you get in a round. I say "get in" because Rancho Park is infamous for the six-plus hours it usually takes to complete eighteen holes.

The course is situated in the heart of Century City right off the main drag. Across the street is 20th Century Fox Studio, where I'd spent four years filming *Charlie's Angels*. Every time I drove to work on Pico Boulevard, the same thing happened. The traffic light that led to the studio would turn red, and I'd glance to the left. I'd see golfers playing; it looked enjoyable, being outside and walking in the fresh air, but I never really thought about going in. The light would turn green, and I'd make a right turn into the studio and go to work. Who knew that one day I'd join their ranks and go from sitting at that red light to standing in the red tees? (*Tee boxes have three areas to tee off from, red, white, and blue. Men usually use the blue and whites while token chicks use the reds.*)

Driving to the course on that first day, I was definitely excited. Pico Boulevard was now the ultimate two-way street. The right had my adventures from *Charlie's Angels*, and the left, new adventures to begin at Rancho Park. The old 'hood would never be the same.

When we pulled into the parking lot, we saw wall-to-wall golfers—at the putting green, hanging outside the clubhouse, and zooming by in their carts. I looked over at Brian, and his eyes were spinning. He was home. We walked into the pro shop, and like many couples, Brian made a beeline for the latest golf clubs on display and I went directly to check out the clothes. Token chicks can never pass up an opportunity to slap the racks. Woops! Except this one! One look

I'd see golfers playing; it looked enjoyable, being outside and walking in the fresh air, but I never really thought about going in.

and I remembered why golf had never interested me. Today it's a different story. Golf clothes have style.

I'm here with Champions Tour player Gary McCord. Besides being one of the most colorful broadcasters in golf, he's also one of the best dressed. I covet his $400 slacks. He's got as much style as any token chick!

Some people feel that the biggest improvement in golf over the last twenty years has been technology: golf balls that fly forever and clubs that are more forgiving than a man of the cloth. However, if you ask me, the biggest improvements go in this order: clothes first, technology second. Thank goodness companies woke up and started designing hip golf clothes or else we'd still be wearing bright yellow polyester pants and pullover sweaters with little golfers sewn on them.

After a brief tour of the merchandise, we approached the man behind the counter, commonly known as the *starter.* He's the one who gets you on the course; he's the one who pairs you with strangers; he's the one who will always tell it like it is.

"First time out?"

Brian answered him, "Ahh, no. I'm Scottish." The starter actually looked somewhat impressed, as if he were thinking,

Maybe this guy does play—he's from Scotland. Then Brian asked if they had rental sets for us to use.

"What's the matter, leave your clubs in Scotland?"

The starter can spot a beginner from a fairway away. He politely asked us, bordering on suggesting, bordering on insisting, "Would you both like to hit balls at the driving range and warm up before you get on the course?"

Brian looked at him like this made no sense. *Warm up*? He said, "I don't need to warm up. I'm Scottish. We just get out there and play."

"What about the lady?"

"Since she's married to a Scot, she follows many of our customs. Like not needing to warm up."

No warm-up? He gave us that classic OK-you-asked-for-it look. We took our clubs, bought golf balls (not nearly enough) and gloves. We got our cart and headed directly for the first tee.

Or so we thought. We actually headed for the tenth tee. Not reading the sign that says *First Tee This Way* is a very common mistake rookies make. The foursome on the tenth tee could tell we were beginners. The golf bags on our cart with the giant tags screaming "RENTAL" combined with driving up to the tenth tee was all they needed to see. With perfect synchronization, the moment we pulled up to their tee box, they lifted their arms, pointed, and said in unison, "The first tee is over there."

On the first tee, Brian tried to recall everything his father had taught him and proceeded with my first lesson. He showed me how to grip the club, how to stand, and how to swing. In the moments leading up to my first tee shot, I had no fear. I'd played all kinds of sports growing up in South Dakota and was a pretty fair athlete. I held my own against the neighborhood boys in softball and basketball, so I didn't give this a second thought.

I teed up my ball, took my stance, adjusted my grip, swung through, and missed the ball by a country mile. I actually heard the *whiff* sound as my club passed in front of me.

Not reading the sign that says **First Tee This Way** is a very common mistake rookies make.

OK, regroup. Deep breath.

On my next swing, I was determined to hit the ball. I figured I just hadn't swung hard enough or fast enough on the first swing. That was why I missed it. I took my stance again, gripped the club even tighter, and swung so hard and fast that the momentum nearly threw me over. This was followed by three more rapid-fire swings, each one not even coming close. I was beginning to realize that golf is a hard game after all.

Regroup—again.

I put some thought into why I could not hit this ball. My mind was thinking one thing, and my body was doing another. My mind was thinking hit the ball as far as I can, and my body was just swinging with reckless abandon. I tried to put it into a mental perspective. "OK, it's just like T-ball, only the ball is at your feet and it's the size of a grape."

I hit a rocket of a tee shot straight down the middle of the fairway. That feeling of striking the ball was like nothing I'd ever felt before.

Then on the sixth swing, the ball finally got off the tee. Not by the swing I had just laid on it, but by the gust of wind I created from missing it again. *Whhiiifff…*

Finally, Brian stepped in. He had to. He couldn't take it anymore. My Scottish knight made some quick adjustments to my stance and grip and gave me a kiss on the cheek. I took a deep breath, pulled the club back, and fired it through. Technically speaking, I crushed it.

I hit a rocket of a tee shot straight down the middle of the fairway. That feeling of striking the ball was like nothing I'd ever felt before. The sound it made, the feeling through my body, and the rush of watching the ball soar out there was almost too much to handle. Good thing it all happened in less than three seconds. As Brian walked back to his tee box, I looked at him now as much more than a husband. He was now the greatest golf teacher in the world!

Brian teed up and smashed his ball down the middle of the fairway too. I started wondering about the Scottish credo he was talking about in our kitchen. I thought, "Maybe he does have a God-given talent." Then I looked at my ball sitting in the middle of the fairway and thought, "Hey, maybe I do too!"

That was all I needed to be totally hooked. One shot. I was now golf's newest life member. There's a feeling about golf we all share. You can hit a hundred bad shots, but it only takes one good shot to bring you back again and again. I hit at least a hundred bad shots the remainder of the day, but I still had that first opening drive.

The wonderment I felt from my first good shot lasted only until I hit my second shot. That's when I cursed for the first time on a golf course. It's not in my nature to use foul language, but it was almost like a reflex. I hit a stinky shot and out came stinky words. I may not have looked like a golfer out there, but I sure was sounding like one.

The conversation in the car driving home was also new to us. Brian and I communicated like never before. We'd stop at a red light, gaze into one another's eyes, and say things like, "Can you believe that putt I made on sixteen!" "Great putt, how about my drive on the last hole!" It was puppy love for us. We were both smitten by the golf bug. We entered the house and immediately planned our next round. We were so exhilarated, it was as if we had just downed a Starbucks Venti drip.

On the way home after our second round, we made a pit stop and bought our first sets of golf clubs. On the way home from our third round, we made another pit stop and bought a condo on a golf course in Palm Springs. It was golf's equivalent of a one-two-three punch.

Rancho Park would also be the course where I would throw my very first club. Not from frustration; that would come later. I threw this club with class, very ladylike. How does one throw a club *ladylike*? Easy. It came from pure innocence.

Brian had shown me a tip that was in his new stack of golf magazines which were now invading my coffee table. This tip was about how much pressure you should apply to your grip when holding a golf club. After you start playing golf, you begin a never-ending quest for tips from every golf magazine that passes before your eyes. Each tip makes perfect sense—as long as you hit the ball well. The second you hit a shot poorly using the new tip, it's the first thing you blame.

This is before I realized how important protection from the sun is. Golfers shouldn't forget to wear sunblock and not expose too much of their skin during their round. You want to be golfing for many years to come, so take care of your skin.

This tip said that you should hold the club gently, as if you were holding a bird. It said to squeeze the club just enough to keep the bird from flying away, but not enough to hurt it. I was practicing at the driving range on the second tier when I decided to put the tip into action. I teed up a ball and gripped my driver as if I were holding a bird. *Gently*. I swung the club and sent my driver flying a hundred yards down the middle of the range! I guess I held it a little *too* gently.

Brian was to my right hitting balls, so he didn't actually see me launch my driver. He only saw the club sailing through the air. He turned around and looked at me. He knew. With a slight cock of his head and an already understanding smile, he asked, "How's it going, honey?"

My hands covering my face answered for me.

Brian asked, "That wasn't your driver, was it, honey?"

"Uh-huh. Now what am I going to do?"

There's nothing you can do in that situation. Word that someone had just flung her driver downrange spread faster than a bad movie review. Within seconds of my driver becoming an airborne projectile, a voice came over the PA system.

"Will everyone please stop hitting balls so a club can be retrieved? Thank you."

While someone fetched my club, I was treated to everyone else staring me down. Some glared, while others pointed. Most just stared. They were all thinking the same thing. "Thank goodness, that wasn't me."

During that summer, I played a lot of golf at Rancho Park. Sometimes in Hollywood the best jobs you get are by word of mouth; golf was going to be no different. Somebody who had seen

> *Golf was the language we spoke on the course. It's universal.*

me playing regularly at Rancho Park told somebody, and that somebody called me with a request: was I interested in playing in a pro-am at an LPGA tournament? *Yeaaahhh* . . . I was paired with a Japanese player who did not speak a word of English, and I don't know if you know this about me, but I don't speak a word of Japanese. When it comes to golf though, it didn't matter. Golf was the language we spoke on the course. It's universal. Smiles, high fives, and the occasional fist pump are as real as any spoken words. I had such a great time participating in that first tournament. I enjoyed the atmosphere of competition. There were people in the galleries watching and interacting with me, someone was carrying my bag—it was just like I had seen on television, and now it was happening to me.

After that first event, I was invited to one pro-am after another. Requests came from everywhere. If I was at a tournament, I would be asked if I wanted to play in another one; some requests came through my agent, and some folks just tracked down my number and phoned me up at home.

Each person who called with a request had a similar comment. "We hear that you have a great time at the tournaments, and the fans really enjoy seeing you out there." That was amazing to hear. People were actually talking about me as a *golfer*. Not as a mom or as an actress, but as a golfer. It was something I had never thought about in my life before, but suddenly it was as important as everything else. One tournament director said "Cheryl, I hear you can always pull a par out of your pocket when the team needs one." I liked that comment the best of all. I am one of those people who tries to be there for my family, my friends, and, of course, for my pro-am team!

People were actually talking about me as a golfer. Not as a mom or as an actress, but as a golfer.

That fall the token chick would be officially born. I got the call from upstairs. Not *that* upstairs. It was an invitation to play in a pro-am event at a PGA tournament. I'd be playing alongside living sports legends, Fortune 500 executives, my favorite actors, and the best professional golfers in the world. Oh yeah, one more thing—this new world was also *all* men. Suddenly the pro-am invitations that were now coming my way had me as the only female celebrity participating. Every tournament was filled with

Armed with fourteen clubs, a good short game, and a sense of humor, the token chick had arrived.

celebrities, male celebrities. That's when I realized who I was, who I had become, my new identity. I was the *token chick.* She became my alter ego, almost like a superhero. "Have no fear, Token Chick is here! I'll make our team's birdie, and you buy the beer!"

What a long way I'd come from the days at Rancho Park. Armed with fourteen clubs, a good short game, and a sense of humor, the token chick had arrived.

TOKEN TIPS

If I could do one thing over, I would take lessons before ever setting foot on a golf course. I played for a while before I took a real lesson and gave myself poor swing habits that took some time to break. When you are out there and don't know what you're doing, nothing good can come of it. Just take a lesson. And not from your friend who says she knows how to play, but from a real golf teacher. Most golf courses have beginner classes on the weekends and even offer beginner classes for women only. A beginner class gives you an immediate sense of the game, and you'll be with players on your level. That's good for your mental confidence in the beginning. What if you have no clubs? Easy. The driving range will have clubs for you to use. But if you are seriously thinking about playing, I suggest getting a ladies' starter set. They come with golf clubs and a bag—everything you need to get going. You can find starter sets in any sporting goods or golf store. What I don't recommend is starting out using your husband's clubs. If you do, chances are you won't hit the ball very well. You will get discouraged quickly, never take up the game, hold some grudge against me, and use my book for kindling. Men's golf clubs are for men. They wear boxers, we wear thongs. Therefore, we need clubs made for women. However, if you're tall, strong, and athletic, you may play well with men's clubs.

TOKEN TIPS continued

Baby steps. Don't expect miracles in the beginning. Try to laugh off bad shots and don't get angry or swing twice as hard the next time. One of the first lessons you learn in golf is self-deprecating humor. So what if you hit a bad shot? You're going to hit plenty in your life, trust me. My favorite story about this comes from Arnold Palmer (who is still sexy, but I'll get to that later in the book). He was playing at Rancho Park (just like me) and scored a twelve on one hole (just like me). A reporter asked him, "How did you make a twelve?" Arnie replied, "I missed a putt for an eleven."

Check out the evolution of my swing. Not to mention my golf clothes. This first shot shows from my finish position that my shoulders are leaning back; therefore my weight is finishing back as well. This is a common problem with beginners. All my weight is still behind me, which means, among other things, less distance. This finish is mostly due to a lack of weight transfer.

TOKEN SIDE TIP If you can't laugh at yourself, this sport's not for you. Put the book down before you wrinkle any more pages and give it to someone as a gift.

Here I'm finishing in a better position with my weight. You can practically draw a straight line down my body and left leg. All my weight has transferred properly, as you can see by the position of my left foot. But you'll also see that I'm not completing my follow-through, which is fine on some shots, but on a tee shot, you want to give it your all, and a full finish means that you've put every ounce of strength into it.

This last picture was taken when my swing and my golf attire were at their finest. Everything in this swing is fundamentally sound. My weight has transferred fully to my left side, I'm facing the target, I've made a complete shoulder turn to finish my swing, and my right foot is pushing off while my left foot is bracing the weight transfer. Also, the line from my shoulder to my foot is perfectly straight. Just think, that nice picture-perfect swing only took me twenty years to get!

MY SECOND BUICK

The year was 1997. Women's golf was making headlines again, Annika Sorenstam was a rising star, and the LPGA was looking toward brighter days. Tiger Woods, Justin Leonard, and Davis Love III all won their first major championships, and I won a major as well. A major to me. It was my official arrival. And what better way to arrive than in a Buick.

As a teenager in the late sixties, I learned how to drive in my father's Buick. It was a blue four-door Le Sabre, no power steering, and it was bigger than a tank. Dads, not little sixteen-year-old girls in South Dakota, should be the only ones allowed to drive that kind of a car. I did a good job behind the wheel, considering that I sat on a pillow to see out the windshield. The main problem I had came from trying to parallel park that monster. I'd slip off the pillow when I turned around trying to back up into a spot. If I was out and wound up somewhere that didn't have a parking spot I could just pull into, I'd have to go somewhere else.

Eventually after a little practice, a few dozen bounced curbs, and two mangled hubcaps, I got the hang of it. My hands shook every time I pulled up to a parking spot, but I eventually got comfortable and the shaking stopped.

The next time my hands were shaking from nerves like that also involved a Buick. It was my second Buick. The 1997 Buick Classic. No, not the sedan—I'm referring to the golf tournament.

My agent called and said that a request had come in from Buick. My immediate thought was that they wanted me to play in one of their pro-ams. Actually, that was my second thought. My first thought was about the parallel parking. I asked him if it was about playing in one of their tournaments; he said, "Sort of." He sounded like someone who was keeping a great secret surprise. He sounded *genuinely* excited for me. He sounded *genuinely* happy for me. He didn't sound like an agent. He sounded like someone who knew that something I would love to be a part of was about to come my way.

"Do they want me for a commercial?"

"In a way they do. Cheryl, they want *you*. Write down this number and call it now. Someone's waiting."

"Who's waiting?"

"Call me when you're through . . . hee hee hee!"

OK, he sounded way too excited. I called the number and spoke with the general manager of Buick, Bob Coletta. A real big wheel. No pun intended.

"Nice to talk to you."

We want you to be our golfing angel.

"You too, Cheryl. Do you know what I wanted to talk to you about?"

"No idea. But my agent must. I've never heard him so excited. Is this a request to play in a pro-am?"

"Better."

"You want me to play in a pro-am, *and* you're also giving me a Buick?"

"Better still. We want you to be our golfing angel."

"Okaaayy—"

What does that mean? I played along as if I knew.

"Of course, your golfing angel."

"Cheryl—" He knew I had no idea what he meant by golfing angel.

"*Yes*—"

"Cheryl, Buick wants you to be on our golf team. We'd like to sponsor you to represent us at tournaments!"

Pause. Gulp! What? Sponsor? As in, "I'm going to wear a cap with the name of a huge company that I'm representing on the golf course"—that kind of a sponsor!

"You want to be my sponsor? Why?"

"Simple. We're looking for a female presence on the pro-am golf circuit who is not a professional golfer. We want someone who has game and whom people know and like. There's one person who fits that bill. You. We want you to be our golfing angel."

I was actually tongue-tied; I said the first thing that came to mind. "Ahh, you know, I learned how to drive in a Buick."

"You see, it's a natural fit."

It certainly was. The official car of the PGA tour was going to be *my* official sponsor! They even had an official title designated for me, Buick Golf Ambassador. Wow! It sounded so cool. Buick Golf Ambassador. When you're in business with an automobile giant, everything they do sounds like a new model car. Take my title for instance: the Buick Golf Ambassador. It sounds like a stylish sports car geared toward golfers. Two seats, convertible, with enough trunk room for two sets of clubs. The Buick Golf Ambassador . . . coming soon! That title almost sounded as if I was going to be working for the United Nations. I asked what my duties were as the official golf ambassador for Buick. "We'd need you to play in the pro-ams at our four PGA tournaments each year, the Buick Invitational, the Classic, the Open, and the Challenge. Socialize with the PGA pros and the amateurs who participate in the events. You'll attend the dinners and cocktail parties we have at each stop, sign autographs, and be very fan friendly. You will be living the life of a famous tour pro without ever having to worry about making the cut each week. What do you think?"

This is the only job that you don't mind going to when it rains.

I played in the pro-am with Billy Mayfair at one of the Buick Opens. I put some pictures in to show you that I'm not all talk about my golf swing. It can stand up to pressure pretty well. Look at this first picture of Billy checking out my 5-iron swing on a par 3. I have a full shoulder turn, my back is completely to the target, weight on my right foot, and a nice bend in my left knee to generate a little more power.

As I move into the ball, you can see that I'm in a great position. My weight has fully transferred to my left foot, and I'm pushing off a little with my right foot. My left arm is straight, and my right hand and arm are steering and driving my clubhead into the ball. When you put a good swing on a ball, you know it the moment you begin your take-away. Professionals can spot a good swing a mile away. That's why I'm really proud of this photo. As you notice, I haven't even made contact with the ball, and Billy is already watching for it to land. Since he saw me start with a good takeaway, he knew that a good swing would follow. I think some of my proper swing mechanics may have rubbed off on Billy that afternoon. He went on to win the Buick Open that weekend.

"Umm, where do I sign up?" After that description, I was ready to pay them. I'd be attending golf fantasy camp. I would not only be the first non-golfer that Buick would sign, but also the first female. They literally wanted me to be their token chick.

Buick sponsored me for four years. I had the time of my life living out the fantasy of being a touring golfer. First-class airfare, fancy hotels, free golf balls—what more could I want? Buick also knows how to treat a lady. They had special pro-ams on Mondays that were for women amateurs only! Just the girls getting to play with the pros. A few of the PGA players definitely preferred these ladies-only pro-ams to the usual ones with the corporate guys. I've played with them in both formats and could see it firsthand. Some pros just had more fun playing with the women. Let's face it: we are a little easier on the eye than the average corporate male they would normally be paired with.

The women also didn't take everything on the course as seriously as the men. We were there to have fun, not win side bets. Some pro-am men take the game too seriously on the course. It can cost big bucks to play in a pro-am, and they would waste the once-in-a-lifetime experience by having a sour puss. I could never understand it. Some of them were so intimidated by playing in the same group with a professional that it would throw their game completely out of whack. If they weren't playing particularly well that day, a lot of them couldn't shake it off. They would get angry with themselves on the course and put the rest of the group in a bad mood as a result.

Great golfer, great guy

I always wanted to walk up to them in the parking lot after the round and say, "Hey, cheer up. Do you honestly think if you played better in front of Davis Love he would suggest that you quit your day job and turn pro?"

Question: What do you call it when you put a bunch of golf-crazed women out on the course with professional male golfers? *Monday Madness!*

This brings me to Ben Crenshaw.

I loved being partnered with him and have always loved watching him play on television because he is *real.* He's not one to hide his feelings about anything. He has the most genuine laugh of anyone I've ever met, and he's a man who is not afraid (or even bashful) about crying. Heck, his wife, Julie, says he cries when the national anthem is played at their daughter's softball games. Ben's especially smooth with the Monday morning pro-am women. He has a suave Texas accent and loves to chat it up with all the girls on the putting green, giving a tip and a compliment jumbled into one sentence.

"You want to feel the putter head during your stroke—that is a beautiful outfit you're wearing."

The emotional energy from losing the man who had shaped his life and winning the Masters was too much for Ben to handle.

"I will do that—and thank you."

Brian and I love watching golf on television. It goes with the territory. If the United States is playing Europe in the Ryder Cup overseas on their turf, we're up at 5 A.M. watching the broadcasts. Before I ever met Ben, Brian and I were glued to the TV watching him win the 1995 Masters tournament. That win was probably one of the most emotional victories in all of sports. (Actually, for me it's a tie with the 1999 Ryder Cup, when the American team had the greatest comeback win in sports history. That team was captained, by, ahh, Ben Crenshaw! What a coincidence.) If you didn't see his second Masters victory, I'll give you the quick details. Ben's mentor, his golf teacher, his greatest influence in life, the legendary Harvey Pennick, had passed away the week before the tournament. Ben served as a pallbearer at the funeral then gathered up all his emotional strength and arrived in time to compete in the Masters. He wanted to play this tournament in honor of his lost leader. Four days later, at age fourty-three, Ben birdied the seventieth and seventy-first holes to defeat Davis Love III and win the Masters by one stroke. After his winning putt fell, Ben fell to his knees and wept uncontrollably. The emotional energy from losing the man who had shaped his life *and* winning the Masters was too much for Ben to handle. It was also too much for Brian and me to handle. His tears and our tears just poured out. We were completely in the zone with him. My teenage daughter walked in the living room and saw us sitting on the couch with tears running down our cheeks. She panicked.

"What's wrong? What happened!"

Brian and I pointed to the television, where Ben was sobbing as uncontrollably as we were.

She looked at the TV and then looked at us.

"Do you know him?"

"No."

"Then why are you both crying?"

We were too choked up to speak. We just kept sniffling. She said, "He's a golfer."

"We know."

"Get a grip."

What can I say? She likes basketball.

"Get a grip."

Ben's professional career started in 1973, and he did something that few have ever accomplished. He won in his first professional tournament. Not only that, it was the San Antonio Texas Open. What else would you expect from a Texan? Winning his first time out and in his home state. He had a very special and personal gallery that followed him around those early years: young, beautiful women. Yes, golf groupies. They were affectionately called "Ben's Wrens," and they followed every step he took on the golf course.

Twenty-plus years later, Ben's Wrens were back. It was at one of the famous Monday Madness all-women pro-am events.

Ben equals Fun. Ben equals Sexy. Ben equals Rugged. Ben equals *Dancer*?

Ben and I were paired with three local women for the tournament. Ben's game was absolutely on fire that afternoon. He was making birdie after birdie, and the women and I were just enjoying watching every stroke of his genius. Ben was eight under par, and the other women and I were about eighty over par. We didn't care, we were having too much fun to focus on golf that day. We became Ben's *New* Wrens! We were his official cheerleaders for the afternoon. Every hole, every shot, we had him going with our made-up high school cheers. None of us remembered any cheerleader dance moves though, so we used a backup. The cabbage patch dance: you swirl your arms in a circle and sway your hips back and forth. It's a lovely dance. Nevertheless, I only recommend it for use at sporting events and not at a wedding.

At the seventeenth hole, Ben's New Wrens (that's us!) had perfected their cabbage patch dance timing. It's all about good timing. Ben's swing was in perfect timing that day—the least the girls and I could do was sync up our cabbaging with our patching.

On that hole, the gallery took our lead, joined in with us, and started a mass cabbage patch epidemic. It was like watching the wave go across a baseball stadium. Walking down the fairway,

Ben said, "I think more golfers would thrive if they had cheerleaders. It works in football."

The cabbage patch dance: you swirl your arms in a circle and sway your hips back and forth.

"Sorry we only know the one dance, but at the next tournament we may have a few surprise cheers for you."

"I may have a surprise for my cheerleaders on the next tee."

"What is it?"

Ben grinned, "You'll see."

We arrived at the eighteenth and the other Wrens and I got into our cheerleader positions right in front of the gallery. We started the cabbage patch moves, and just like at the previous hole, the crowd was joining in. Ben watched the scene while he was taking a few warm-up swings, then dropped his club to the ground and got right in the middle of our cheerleader squad. He started swirling his hips and moving his arms and was in full-blown cabbage patch mode. The gallery went nuts! They all started screaming, "Go Ben! Go Ben! Go Ben!"

Ben danced like he had just been schooled by Bob Fosse.

"Go Ben! Go Ben!"

Ben's face was positively glowing. He had played an amazing round all day and treated himself to a little fun before his last tee shot. After our troupe's initial bow and one curtain call later, Ben stood on the tee ready to hit his shot. He even gave one more little hip swirl before he teed off. His last hip swirl gave the crowd one last laugh; he teed off and, not surprisingly, found the center of the fairway. As we walked down the last fairway together, Ben was still moving his hips and arms a little. Now he was working the gallery that lined the fairway. He said to me, "I may have to work this cabbage patch dance into my regular warm-up routine."

Whenever I see Ben on television being interviewed or playing, I just think to myself, "Great golfer, great guy."

Buick also gave me my first opportunity to meet Tiger Woods. (Tiger hadn't yet signed with Buick; that would happen in 1999.) I knew that our paths would probably cross at one of the Buick-sponsored events. I went zero for four in 1997. Tiger had won the Masters that year and the golf world—who am I kidding, the *whole* world—was in the throes of Tigermania.

Everyone wanted to meet him. At Warwick Hills Golf and Country Club in Grand Blanc, Michigan, Wednesday, August 6, 1998, during the pro-am at the Buick Open, my chance would come. There was a huge crowd gathered around the eighteenth hole, and that could only mean one thing: a Tiger was on the prowl.

I stalled everyone in my group a bit and waited for my chance. For a woman golfer hoping to meet Tiger, it was the new millennium version of Elvis's train passing through your town. Tiger and I had a brief talk, all of which is a blur to me now. I was so nervous talking to him that I don't even remember saying anything other than, "You're great." I did manage to hold it together long enough to suggest that we exchange golf balls. I gave him one that was stamped "Cheryl Ladd," and he gave me one of his, infamously stamped "TIGER."

The next day my little meeting with Tiger was on the front page of the sports section. Talk about a great way to get your husband to give you three dozen roses! I don't think he was jealous—I think he wanted me to give him Tiger's golf ball.

When I signed my Buick contract, I felt like I was Tiger Woods or an athlete who has just been chosen as the number one draft pick. I signed, we shook hands, there were pictures taken, and they gave me my first cap with BUICK emblazoned across the front. Slight confession time: I loved wearing my cap in tournaments. Don't laugh! It made me feel so good. I know that someone, somewhere, is going to rib me about this one day, but when I was in a tournament and I put on my golf clothes and then my officially sponsored cap, it felt like Supergirl's cape. I'd morph into my token chick mode and fire at every flag. I wouldn't hit every green, but I would always go for it. My years with Buick were a blast.

When I signed my Buick contract, I felt like I was Tiger Woods

Thankfully, I don't need to play golf in order to earn a living, or else I'd starve. However, in Bob Coletta's own words on the phone that first day with me, it all fit. That's not always the case out on tour with getting a sponsor.

Thankfully, I don't need to play golf in order to earn a living, or else I'd starve.

One of the first important steps for golfers who turn pro is locking up a sponsor. You've probably seen big bright company logos on a pro's bag, hat shirt, or shoes. Even the watch a golfer wears can be sold for substantial sums to a willing sponsor. The dollars these sponsors provide to young pros can be the difference in making or breaking a career. That extra money helps take the load off weekly travel expenses, a caddy, and a lot of take-out pizzas. And even if you're a proven player, it's still hard to get sponsored. I'll give you an example. One of my favorite players to watch on the LPGA tour is Meg Mallon. Maybe you've heard of her, maybe you haven't. At the time I am writing this, she has amassed eighteen victories in her seventeen years on tour. On the 4th of July 2004, a few months after turning forty-one, Meg won her second U.S. Women's Open. I was watching in my living room, but I was hardly glued to my couch—I was jumping up and down too much. On that afternoon, Meg was solid as a rock. She had the number one player in the world, Annika Sorenstam, making her usual Sunday charge. Meg would not falter though. She had an historic round that Sunday by shooting a final round score of sixty-five. It was the lowest final round ever in the history of the Women's U.S. Open. She had it all going on Sunday—good fortune and sweet putting.

One thing Meg *didn't* have on Sunday was a sponsor on her cap. Can you believe that? She's a future Hall of Fame player, a staple on the LPGA tour, but the cap she wore that week was the standard issue U.S. Open hat that she bought in the pro shop. She had a record-breaking month in the world of sports, yet most people wouldn't know it.

After winning the U.S. Open, she went on to win the following week as well, becoming only the third player in LPGA history to win a tournament the week after winning the U.S. Open. It wasn't just any tournament either; it was the Canadian Open. The national championship for Canada. No woman has ever won the Canadian Open and the U.S. Open in the same year. In case you're curious about the men, only two players have done it: Lee Trevino and Tiger Woods. That's good company to keep. Yet no sponsor for a player of this caliber? I've seen plenty of television commercials with famous basketball or football players or other athletes who either currently are or have been in trouble with the law, their family, or their team. Yet they continue to reap the benefits of having multimillion-dollar endorsement deals.

I met Meg and played nine holes with her at one of the Buick events. I found her to be—and this is a good thing—very normal.

I was talking to Brian that night on the phone and remember telling him, "I played with Meg Mallon today. I've been in a great mood ever since." Have you ever met someone or had a friend who was able to spread *their* good vibe your way? Meg is one of those types.

I feel that an athlete like Meg is a great role model and should have sponsors up to her ears. Or even above her ears—like on the front of her cap. Not long after those wins, Meg got a sponsor (and an excellent one at that) on her cap. But there is always room for more on her shirt. Now, if anyone at Buick is reading this, I think Meg also learned how to drive in a Buick. You should give her a call. *Wink, wink . . .*

TOKEN TIPS

Ben Crenshaw, Tiger Woods, and Meg Mallon are all superb putters. I remember seeing an interview with Tiger where he talked about approaching Ben while he was practicing his putting. I did the same thing and asked Ben for a lesson on the basics. Here it is.

1

First, position the ball off the inside of your left foot.

2

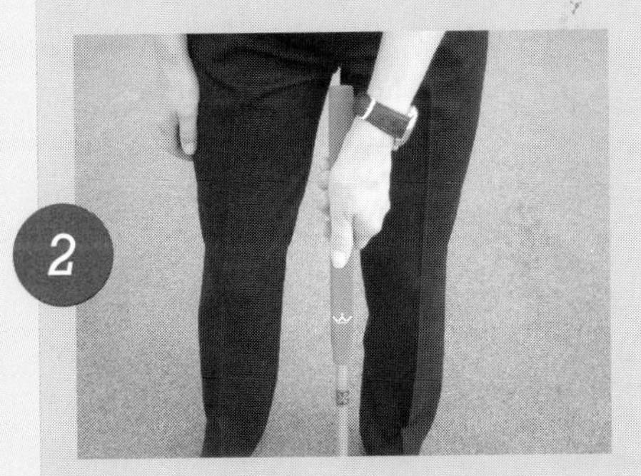

Next comes a good grip. There are several ways, but Ben showed me the one that's most common. It's called the reverse overlap. Sounds hard, but it couldn't be easier. Grip the club with your left hand and run it along the seam of your palm. Place your thumb so that it's pointing straight down the center of the shaft.

continued

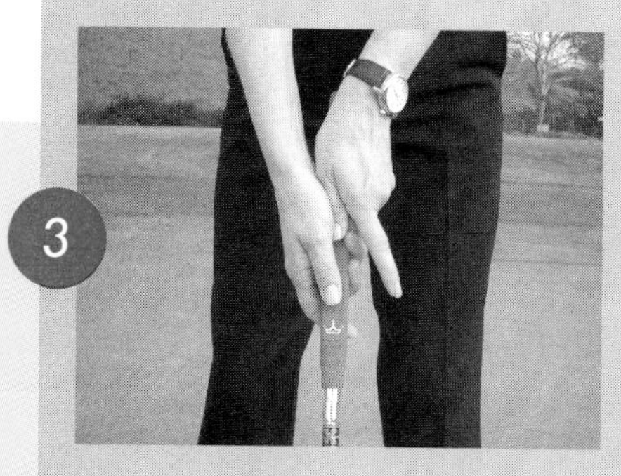

Here's where the reverse overlap comes in. Lift your index finger off the grip and allow the right hand to fit snugly beneath the left.

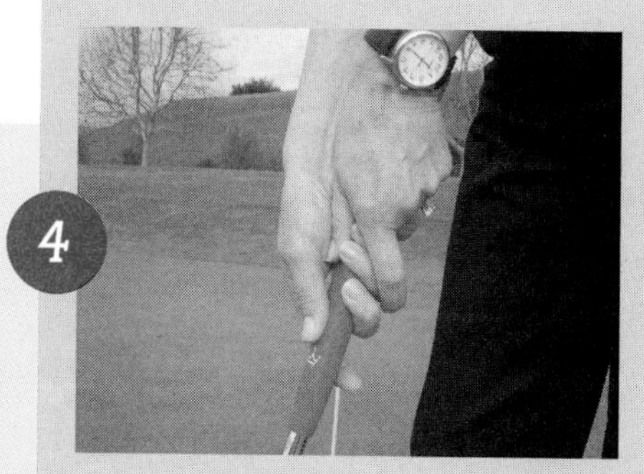

Then place your left index finger across the fingers on your right hand.

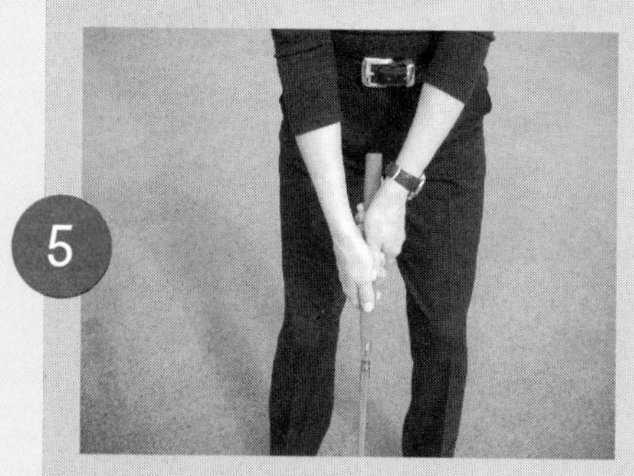

Both your thumbs should now be positioned down the grip. You'll notice I choke down on my putter. They come in different lengths and I suggest that token chicks get a putter that's either 33 or 34 inches long. My putter is a standard men's length, 35 inches. I have putters that are shorter, but I like the weight of a longer putter and I also like to choke down on the putter. But that's me; you may be completely different.

The putter department in the golf store has every putter imaginable for you to try, so check them all out. Ben also stresses maintaining the same grip pressure throughout your stroke. You don't want to choke the putter, and you don't want it too loose either. It should be firm enough so that when you stroke the putter back, the head of the club stays in sync with your arms. If you're holding the putter too loosely, it'll look like this.

Now how should you stand? Some people like their legs far apart, some like them the same width as their shoulders, and others like them close together. Use whatever works best for you. But something we should all have in common is proper putting posture. You don't want to be too hunched over the ball . . .

. . . and you don't want to be too erect.

You want to bend at your hips and allow your arms to hang freely.

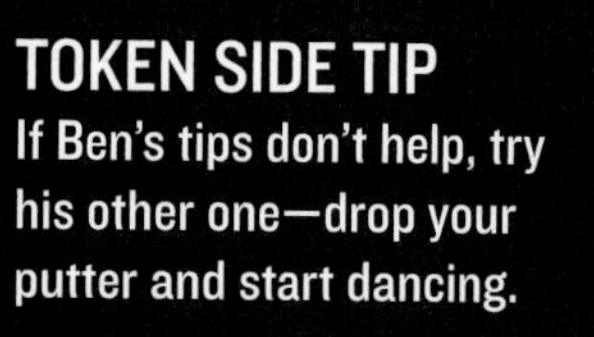

TOKEN SIDE TIP
If Ben's tips don't help, try his other one—drop your putter and start dancing.

And lastly comes the stroke. You want to move only your shoulders and keep your body still. Don't sway back with the putter. Your body needs to serve as an anchor when you putt. I also recommend holding your finish on each putt, even your practice strokes. Holding the finish will help you develop a fluid stroke.

INSPIRATION

Golf is 90 percent mental and 10 percent mental.

Nothing sums it up better. It's all in the head. The biggest obstacle in golf is . . . *your mind.* Great players are great because they're able to block out bad thoughts and distractions and use inspiration to guide them. It's the second thing that separates us hackers from the professionals, the first obviously being their swings. Confidence is the fifteenth club in their bag. The fifteenth club in *our* bag is a water ball retriever.

And it's not as if we can't follow their lead and use inspiration when we play. It's as easy as whipping up a protein shake before an early-morning round. Inspiration comes in different ways on the golf course. A good "swing thought," always staying positive, and knowing there's a great snack stand between the ninth and tenth holes are good starters.

One player who stands out in my mind about staying positive is Davis Love III. Davis was born with golf in his veins. His father and mentor, Davis Love, was a renowned and respected golf teaching professional. I'll tell you an interesting piece of Davis Love trivia. I'm sure you've heard of Michael Jordan. If you haven't, *basketball*... OK, now you're with me. When Davis was in college at North Carolina, one of his friends was Michael Jordan. Davis convinced Michael to give golf a whirl one afternoon with him. Michael was hooked from that day on. Nowadays, MJ's days of his blissful retirement are spent cranking out at least thirty-six holes of golf.

On the course playing alongside Davis, I was very intrigued by his positive attitude. Growing up with a golf teacher for a father, Davis understood at an early age that having a strong positive attitude was as important as a strong swing. Whenever I played with him, he would guide me into a positive perspective about the game. If I hit a bad shot, Davis found the positive in it.

"Cheryl, that was a good swing. Your upper body and shoulders really came through on that one—you just hit the ball a little thin. Next time when you address the ball with that club, move the ball back from the front of your stance to more in the middle, and you'll hit it flush every time."

Besides having that positive attitude, there was another reason I enjoyed playing with Davis—he's cute! He's a true gentleman, with boyish Southern charm and a smile that can make any token chick melt. Davis always said that the key to staying positive through your round is to start out that way and maintain a good attitude for your whole round.

Davis always said that the key to staying positive through your round is to start out that way and maintain a good attitude for your whole round.

Some golfers actually start out positive and play a few good holes until they get to the "blowup hole." The blowup hole can be anything from getting a triple bogey to, well, the sky's the limit on the blowup hole! I have personally scored, in succession, par, par, birdie, par, birdie, eleven. *Kaboom!* If this has happened to you, raise your hand. OK, please put your hands down, I can't see anything. Ultimately, if you don't get your emotions under control it can only lead to you selling your "new but hardly used and still in their original factory box" golf clubs on eBay. So when you get out there, always carry a positive attitude. (Also carry a banana; they're a great snack to have on the course.) Remember . . . *90 percent mental, 10 percent mental.*

*A small, intimate group of **five hundred** people gathered at the first tee to help swell my jitters.*

I needed all my mental strength for a tournament in Tucson, Arizona. I was playing in the LPGA pro-am at the Welch's/Circle K tournament at Randolph Park Golf Course. The fairway was lined with trees, and the course was very long, even by LPGA standards. Knowing that I had to hit a long drive on the first tee was *not* the swing thought I needed to start my day. That thought quickly allowed me to get an illness all golfers face. The first-tee jitters. Dizziness, stomach churning, weak legs, anxiety—very much like PMS. A small, intimate group of *five hundred* people gathered at the first tee to help swell my jitters. *Swelling*, just like PMS.

I stood on the tee, and they announced my name. At least I thought they were announcing my name. The first-tee jitters have also been known to affect your hearing. I assumed it was my name since the gallery was looking at me and applauding. I bent down and teed up my ball. I didn't even do that with confidence. The tee I stuck in the ground actually broke when it hit the dirt. I put another tee in the ground, and this time I accidentally knocked the ball off when I was addressing the ball. This was starting to be painful.

I finally teed off. To my surprise, it didn't slice or hook. I should have been so lucky. My drive didn't even travel far enough to gain momentum for it to slice or hook. It went all of fifty yards.

A fifty-yard *snake* shot. You know the one, the ball gets six feet off the ground and then slithers down the fairway. At this point I was ready to go home.

After I hit that tragic opening drive, the gallery had no choice but to pay their respects by bowing their heads and observing a moment of silence. They had manners. They felt my pain. They'd been there. They'd hit those tee shots. Only not in front of five hundred people! There was even a smattering of *sympathy applause.* Nothing is more painful than sympathy applause. I remember walking to my ball—it was a short walk—thinking, "Why am I here, and why do I play golf anyway? It's a beautiful day, I should be in my garden. I'm good at gardening."

Almost on cue, in the midst of this deafening moment of silence, a little girl's voice cried out. More like squeaked out. It was the same type of voice that comes out of a doll when you pull its string: *I love my mommy. I love my mommy.* It was the voice that was created by toy manufacturers to give little girls a sense of security. That voice. My little doll on the golf course squeaked out the words, "That's OK, Cheryl!" The gallery burst out laughing. Out of the mouths of babes . . .

I laughed right along with everyone over her honest, innocent, and funny words of inspiration. I got to my shot and looked down at my ball. *Tragic.* Then I looked at the gallery, laughing and happy. *Magic.* That little girl had turned *tragic* into *magic.* The next time something similar happens to you, remember that bad shots can happen to good people. It's nothing personal, it's just golf.

The next time you are afflicted with first-tee jitters, think about the little girl before you hit your tee shot. "*That's OK, Cheryl!*" That should help ease the jitters a little. If it makes you feel better, please substitute your name for mine. But I say leave it in. It'll make you laugh a little.

We all give inspiration on the course without even realizing it. It's inherent in anyone who has ever picked up a golf club. If someone sinks a putt we say, "Nice putt." If they miss we may say, "You put a nice stroke on it, good effort." Even after a bad round, your partners will offer encouragement.

"I played so lousy today."

"Yeah, but how about that drive you hit on the seventh, or your par-saving putt on the eighteenth? I wish I could putt like that." Whether it's the partner you're paired with for your round or the partner you're paired with for life, golf brings out the best in people.

Brian and I were playing in the pro-am for the Buick Invitational at Torrey Pines in San Diego. They have two of the finest courses you could ever play, and it has been a favorite stop on the PGA tour for over thirty-five years. For amateurs, getting to play on courses that host PGA events is like good homemade gravy. You can

We all give inspiration on the course without even realizing it.

never get enough of it. To play golf on the same courses that the pros play on is just plain *cool*. What other sport offers that? If you play tennis, you know that it's very hard to get court time at Wimbledon. Torrey Pines is a municipal public golf course—in other words, it's open to all of us. No membership or jacket required.

The past winners of the Buick Invitational are Hall of Fame caliber: Palmer, Nicklaus, Player, Watson, Love, Woods, and Ladd. (Thought I'd sneak that in . . . Read on.)

Torrey Pines has a classic golf layout. It's filled with those trees that have nice big leaves and thick trunks and gravitational pull. I think the botanical name for them is *Pine-Needle-Slice-and-Duck-Hook Trees*. Their tree bark attracts the material used in golf balls, so when you tee off most of your shots head straight for the woods. Like a magnet. You may even have a few of these trees at your local course.

In this event, Brian and I were playing on different teams. Each group had a pro golfer or celebrity playing with them. Brian's pro was Billy Andrade. I know Billy pretty well, and there are not enough nice words to say about him. He does plenty of charity work and truly epitomizes all the good that the PGA does.

The touring schedule for the pros is pretty much the same every week. Monday they arrive. Tuesday they practice on their own. Wednesday there is the pro-am where the pros and celebrities play alongside the locals who are living out their golfing fantasy: playing golf alongside a PGA or an LPGA professional.

Brian and Billy Andrade

While the *pro-amers* are enjoying their afternoon on the course, the *pros* are at work. They're learning how the greens break and getting used to completely different course conditions from the previous week's event. Yet most of the time, you'd never know they're at work and that you're actually at *their* job with them. The pros are pondering their strategy for the real tournament, while the pro-amers are pondering how many hats they can get the pros to sign after the round. Imagine if you had a big presentation for your boss early Thursday morning. Very early, like a 6:15 A.M. tee time at your local course. But the day before while you were preparing the presentation at your desk, you had to entertain four strangers for five hours. Make them laugh, eat lunch together, and so on. That's what it is for them, week after week.

In the pro-ams, the pros always tee off first. Since they hit from the back tees, it just makes life easier. Billy teed up his ball and smashed his drive. He hit a missile 285 yards straight down the middle of the fairway. Standing a few feet from a professional hitting a tee shot is something that every golfer needs to experience. And we all can. Every major city around the world has professional tournaments. If you've never been to one, get yourself there the next time they roll into your town.

Standing a few feet from a professional hitting a tee shot is something that every golfer needs to experience.

Since I've played in so many events, I'm accustomed to seeing PGA and LPGA pros launch their balls into orbit. Accustomed?—yes. Amazed?—every time. When you watch Tiger Woods hit a tee shot on television, it looks fantastic, but it's not the same as being there in the flesh. When pros hit the ball with their driver, the sound the clubface makes is startling. Your first instinct is to think that you've been shot with a high-powered rifle. When the amateurs see the pros tee off, their facial reaction is—what do they say in that commercial?—priceless.

I've noticed a trend at pro-ams. When a pro tees off and rips it down the fairway, it generally has one of two effects on the amateurs in the group. Some get inspired and hit the drive of their life. But most of the time they're so freaked out that they send their tee shot sailing into an innocent gallery.

After Billy's textbook drive, the rest of Brian's group teed off. None of their shots was covered in glory. Nothing that even resembled a good miss. Billy was accustomed to seeing this and assumed that everyone would settle down and play steadier as they went on. That's what usually happens anyway. The next

QUICK TOKEN TIP When you go to a pro-am tournament to watch the action, don't stand in the first row of spectators. Basically, you're open game for the amateurs when they tee off. I've seen many fans get hit with every type of shot under the sun. Duck-hooked, sliced, shanked, skulled, thinned, or chunked, there's more than one way to skin a spectator.

three holes were shaky at best. Each guy was dishing up a wide variety of topped tee shots, scooped shots, flubbed two-foot putts, and a nice assortment of chunked chips. (Sounds like an ice-cream sundae for hackers. "I'll have a two-scoop chocolate-flubbed two-foot-putt sundae topped with sprinkles, please.")

Well, it didn't get any better as Billy and Brian and the other guys had hoped. They just kept hitting one bad shot after another. Billy had enough. This was *worse* than normal. He called for a team meeting. Having played in so many pro-ams, Brian knew what was coming next. The typical pep talk he's heard from well-meaning and encouraging pros he's played with in the past. "Try to relax, you guys have talent, it doesn't matter at the end of the day because it's just a game." All that jazz . . .

Brian's team

Billy huddles with his nervous teammates, takes a long, deep breath, and with a straight face says, "Guys, *you suck*! You just suck and that's all there is to it. I want you to know that this is the last pep talk you're getting. *You. Suck.*" Some pep talk! But it worked. Billy's funny words of inspiration did a world of good for Brian's group. They relaxed and put their sucky shots behind them and played lights-out golf the rest of the day. When their round was finished, they were in the lead by three strokes. Victory was at hand.

Even though it seemed like a lock for Brian's team to win, one group was still on the course with a slight chance of overtaking them. That team was none other than my team. Playing in my group was Bob Coletta, general manager of Buick Motors, a truly great guy, and the brilliant Davis Love III. Let me give you the reason why my team had even the slightest chance to win. Davis and Bob. They both played so well that day, while my swing had decided to start heading south for an early winter. Of all the days for this to happen! After all, Davis is one of the best golfers in the world. I was the Buick ambassador, and I'm playing with the head honcho. During the round, I'm sure Bob Coletta must have thought, *Why are we paying this woman to be our golf ambassador?* For a moment, I envisioned someone walking out of a Buick dealership spewing about my golf game and not buying a car because of it. These thoughts were not helping my swing either. But in any event, we still had a chance to win the tournament. The thought of winning a golf tournament at

My team

Torrey Pines is like hitting a grand slam in Yankee Stadium to win the World Series.

Brian and one of his partners were doing a little early celebrating, and they decided to walk the last few holes with my group. As Brian was crossing the fairway on the walk over, he saw me hit my second shot. It was N.G. *Not Good.* I wasn't having a good day at all out there. A lot of fighting going on. Not with my partners, with my swing. We all fight our swing sometimes. Isn't it insane when you think about it? We actually *fight* with our swing. We've all hit bad shots and said under our breath, "C'mon . . ." Are we expecting the swing to answer us, "Are you talking to me? You hit that crummy shot . . . I didn't."

Brian walked over, and he just looked like a winner. I could see on his face that his team had either won or was going to win the tournament. But he didn't say anything about that. He wanted to help me with *my* swing. He'd seen my shot and the problem with it. Since Brian and I play so much together, we can analyze each other's swings in an instant. One look and he said, "Honey, you're not finishing your backswing. You can't get into the slot." When we get into bad swing habits, it's generally hard to fix the problem during a round. Lately, I had developed this *not finishing my swing* habit. It was causing me to push all my shots to the right.

Not finishing my shoulder turn stops me from getting my swing into the slot. You'll hear golfers talk about getting into the slot as if it's some mystical place. (For more on "the slot," see the Token Tips at the end of this chapter.)

You'll hear golfers talk about getting into the slot as if it's some mystical place.

After getting those golden tips from B-man, I stood over my third shot. It was a par 4, and I needed to hit my ball close to the pin. If I could do that and sink the putt, I'd walk away with a natural par on the scorecard. My handicap was giving me one stroke on the hole, so a natural par would give my team that birdie and the one point we desperately needed. I thought about what Brian had told me. Finishing my backswing and getting into the slot. That little tweak gave me the confidence *and* inspired me to knock my third shot stiff. It was no more than two feet from the cup. I walked up there and dropped my putt for par. Please don't forget that I'm getting a stroke on this

hole, so kindly score the token chick with a birdie, thank you. My partner from Buick, OK, my boss, Bob, hit his shot close too, and he also sank his putt for a birdie. Suddenly we were in position to take the tournament. It was coming down to the final hole. For a moment, I thought we might not even make it to the final hole. Brian's partner was about to kill him for giving me the tip that sparked my team.

They say in Hollywood, "You're only as good as your last project." Golf is no different. I had played horribly all day, but give me a strong finish with a birdie that might help my team win, then that's what they'll remember most. Which was fine by me.

My group did indeed go on to win the tournament by that single stroke over

Brian's team. If not for his tips that helped my swing come back north after it had gone south all day, his team would have won. That's the generosity of golf and a loving husband. Brian's group getting that gospel speech from Billy Andrade—"You guys, you suck!"—gave his team the inspiration they needed to start their engines. Brian passed that inspiration right along to me with his quick tips to fix my swing.

It was one of the best days ever on a golf course for both of us. Husband and wife. Or for that day, first- and second-place winners. Not too shabby . . .

Husband and wife. Or for that day, first- and second-place winners.

TOKEN TIPS

I spoke about getting your swing into *the slot*. First, what does that mean?

1

The simple definition is completing your shoulder turn from the halfway back position up to the top of your swing, which puts you in a slot.

TOKEN SIDE TIP If you're playing golf and your mind begins to wander about what to cook for dinner, just decide to pick up a pizza on the way home and get back to focusing on your golf swing.

Is this what Hands On Training means?

This way, when you swing down you're heading into the same position you started in, as if you're swinging inside a slot.

You may be playing well all day and toward the end find that your swing is not getting into the slot. This happens when our minds wander and we're thinking about cooking dinner, picking up the dry cleaning, or any number of distractions that have nothing to do with golf. We get lazy with the swing and don't finish it. We do a half turn back and then lift our arms high, actually faking a full turn. It only fools you, not the golf ball.

GOLF MECCA

Besides giving me the gift of a lifetime by introducing me to golf, Brian gave me the best follow-up too. It was in the fall of 1984 after we had been playing for a few months he suggested that we take our golf games to the next level. Just like when he initially suggested we take up the game, he came to me with that same intensity.

"Cheryl, I want to talk about something. I'm Scottish."

"Here we go again . . ."

"Well, being Scottish, and also now being a Scottish golfer, I think we need to take a trip to the homeland."

"South Dakota?"

"My homeland."

"You mean, Farkil—"

"Falkirk. No, not there, close. St. Andrews."

One week later, we were on a plane to do battle against one of the toughest opponents known to golfers worldwide, the birthplace of the game itself: the Old Course at St. Andrews.

First tee optimism . . . albeit shortlived

We had enough game to get us around our local courses in California, but the Old Course at St. Andrews is a different type of animal. It's a beast. I'd never been intimidated by the sight of land, but this place does it to you. Then again, I'd never stood on land that had been only slightly altered in the last six centuries. St. Andrews is called a "links" golf course. If you've ever seen a British Open on television, these are the types of courses that are used. The expression, "Let's hit the links" was obviously derived from them, but just exactly what does "links" golf mean? There are several definitions, but I feel the easiest one is, the land that *links* with the sea. Links courses are usually built next to a body of water, they have long, tall, whispy grass hazards called *fescue*, very few if any trees, and rolling green and brown hard surfaced fairways that seem to go on for miles in every direction. I looked at the first hole of St. Andrews and the enormous amount of land that stood awaiting me, then looked at the tiny little golf ball in my hand and thought, "I don't stand a chance." When I met the caddy that Brian and I were assigned, it didn't look like we'd even finish one hole. He was at least eighty years old, and if he were living in America, he'd be classified as legally blind. He introduced himself with a disclaimer.

"I know what you're thinking—that I'm old. Well, that's only the half of it. Only one eye works and the other is pretty weak. Makes no difference, I know this place better than anybody does. I've been a caddy here for over fifty years and I know every crevice as well as I know what I like to eat for breakfast."

"Where are you going dear? That's for the big knockers."

"What did you have for breakfast?"

"I don't remember. Shall we head out?"

At the very first tee box, he said something that made me question if he in fact was blind.

"Where are you going dear? That's for the big knockers."

"Big knockers?"

"Yes, the big knockers; not you."

"Excuse me?"

"The big knockers tee it up from the back, ladies knock it from upfront."

Oh, now I get it. I was walking to the wrong tee box. Whew . . . As I was teeing it up, Brian leaned in and whispered in

I appreciated being there and feeling the history of the Old Course, but I made a vow that day to return only when I had more game.

my ear, "I think your knockers are just fine, honey." There's nothing like a little encouragement from your man.

After each shot I hit, the caddy just grumbled. "Acch, Lass, you're in the heather again, Acch, Lass, you're in the bunker again." Some doctors say that when one sense gets weaker the others get stronger. This man was living proof. I don't think he could see twenty feet in front of him, but he could tell you where your ball landed just by the sound it made coming off the clubhead. He could tell if it was going to the right, to the left, if it was high in the air or low to the ground. He was unbelievable.

I can sum up every shot the same way: hit it, watch it roll, and watch it disappear into a six-foot-deep bunker. These aren't sand traps like the ones we're accustomed to in the States. These are like small craters made by exploded bombs and then filled in with sand. The names of these bunkers alone are enough to scare you, The Coffins, Hell Bunker, and the one no one ever wants to be sent to, The Principal's Nose. In total, there are 112 bunkers at St. Andrews, and during my round, I was in almost every one. I learned something very important that day. Never hit into a trap that has a ladder built into it. I appreciated being there and feeling the history of the Old Course, but I made a vow that day to return only when I had more game.

In 1994, Brian and I were invited to Ireland for the opening of the Kildare Hotel and Country Club. Commonly known as the K Club, it's about thirty miles west of Dublin, set on over three hundred acres of woodland. The main estate on the grounds dates back to the year 550. The river Liffey, which has been immortalized in the writings of James Joyce, runs along the grounds along with eleven other lakes. There are two courses, both designed by Arnold Palmer, who describes them as "a blend of pleasure, skill, and challenge." Every year the K Club plays host to the Smurfit European Open. In September of 2006, it is hosting the Ryder Cup, which will be played in Ireland for the first time ever.

Now, one of the best perks of being in show business is a weekend like this. I've been to fantastic events before, but this was a little like Christmas. After a royal-treatment flight overseas on British Airways, Brian and I walked into our hotel room and found it draped in gifts.

Crystal champagne glasses, buttersoft leather luggage sets, perfumes—for a moment I thought they had sent us to the wrong room and maybe these gifts were for a visiting princess. Suddenly there was a knock that I thought came from the door. *Darn!* I thought. *These gifts aren't for us; we are in the wrong room.* Then another knock. And another. But they weren't coming from the door.

I've been to fantastic events before, but this was a little like Christmas.

They were coming from the windows. It was Ireland, and that could only mean one thing. Hard cold rain was suddenly pelting our hotel. We had arrived less than an hour earlier and the skies had been clear the entire trip, but out of nowhere, hail struck with fury.

That night after an exceptional dinner and some superb wine, we went back up to our room to get a good night's sleep for the big tournament the next morning. The rain continued throughout the night, and I was beginning to worry. Not about the weather—I didn't want the new luggage to get ruined by the moisture.

The course was saturated that morning, and when we got there, I didn't think it would be playable. The tournament officials said that there was no way we'd get in eighteen holes, but could we all try and play nine. *No problem.* The weather was treacherous, but I'm telling you the luggage was so gorgeous. I figured playing was the least I could do.

As I arrived at the first tee, I couldn't believe my eyes when I saw how many fans were lining the fairway—just as if the sun was beaming. These were real-life *fighting Irish* in the flesh. A little freezing rain, sleet, and thirty-mile-an-hour winds couldn't keep these diehard golf fans away. My round was just brutal. The wind was so strong that on one hole I'd be unable to swing my club back, and on the next the wind would knock me over as I followed through.

Brian's tee time was about an hour and a half earlier than mine, and he had to deal with the worst of the weather. It felt like being under attack. However, the combination of freezing rain, wind, occasional sleet, and thirty-degree temperatures made for one of Brian's best rounds and one of my favorite stories.

As I arrived at the first tee, I couldn't believe my eyes when I saw how many fans were lining the fairway—just as if the sun was beaming.

His caddy that day could not have been more than thirteen years old, and he had freckles that lit up through the hard, dark rain. Brian walked out of the clubhouse and into the drenching non-stop showers, but the boy caddy had a question before their round began.

"Excuse me, Mr. Russell. The other caddies say that you're married to Cheryl Ladd."

"Yes, I am."

"Well, can I ask you a question?"

"Sure."

"Do you think you could arrange for me to be her caddy today?"

"Not a chance. Grab the bag!"

Before we left California, Brian had been working hard on his chipping. It was the usual weekly routine he follows leading up to every trip we take to Scotland. He would need a lot of short-game skill that morning at the K Club. Besides the rain, the wind was so fierce during his nine holes that no one in his group was able reach a green in regulation, let alone in three or four shots. Brian's chipping that round was the best it's ever been. As the golf announcers say in Europe, his chipping was *majestic.* Every chip left him close enough to the hole to give him a great chance at saving his par. His young caddy was very impressed and he followed every good chip with a compliment.

"That chipper you've got, it's like a magic wand in your hands."

"Mr. Russell, I've never seen anyone chip as well as you."

"That chipper you've got, it's like a magic wand in your hands."

"It's a thing of beauty."

"Tell me, are all Americans as fine a chipper as you?"

This continued hole after hole. Even though the boy sounded sincere, Brian began to wonder if he was being complimented or being hosed. On the final hole, Brian chipped his ball to gimme range, saving another par. The young caddy shook his head in amazement and said, "Mr. Russell, you have to be the finest chipper I've ever seen." "Thanks," Brian said. "By the way, how long have you been a caddy?" The boy grinned with pride and said, "Acch, two weeks, sir."

Whenever we go to Scotland to play, this is Brian's fate. Either he has a caddy who's the older brother of Father Time or a kid who's barely reached puberty. Brian would continue his caddy hot streak at the Machrie golf club. It's situated on the beautiful shores of the whiskey island of Islay. Dating back to 1891, it has a sixteen-bedroom hotel along with a fifteen private cottages. While the course has undergone some minor upgrades, its classic and little-changed design makes you feel like you're playing golf in a page from a history book. For this round in the caddy lottery, Brian drew a red-faced little Scottish boy who had just turned nine. It was such a sight, this little boy carrying a bag that was as tall as he was and enjoying every moment of it. He was definitely new to caddying with probably less experience than the two weeks Brian's previous lad had put in. This adorable little boy would accidentally drop a club during someone's putt or the whole bag altogether when his attention was diverted by a passing butterfly. After every slipup, he came back with apologies and youthful determination.

I knew Brian had really taken a liking to the boy because he couldn't resist teasing him. Brian said to him, "You realize that this is the finest privilege of your young life. Being able to caddy for someone as important as me." Brian looked over and winked at me. I knew. This cute kid was buying into the whole idea that being Brian's caddy was indeed an honor. With a sweet innocent young Scottish brogue, he'd say to Brian, "Oh, Mr. Russell, it is a fine honor to caddy for you. You're the best player I've ever seen." Brian rolled his eyes, looked at me and said, "Here we go again."

At the end of the round, Brian had the lad's tip at the ready, but couldn't resist one last ribbing. He said, "Listen, you've messed up a few times today, but I think you learned a few things about being a caddy too. Therefore, maybe you should be paying me." He soaked in Brian's words and said, "I'm sorry, sir, I can't pay you. I didn't bring my money." He then reached his little hand into his pocket and pulled out half a chocolate bar and a golf ball. He looked up at Brian and with such sincerity he said, "It's all I've got sir, but they're yours if you want them." Brian melted and said to him, "Well you know you didn't do such a bad job after all, this is for you." He gave him a fifty-pound note and the kid nearly fell over. He was really taken aback, "Oh no, Mr. Russell, I can't take this sir." He tried to give it back, but Brian insisted. "No, you take that and remember, try not to drop the bag during someone's backswing." When we were leaving the course, the boy yelled proudly, "Mr. Russell, you know I've been to America. We went to Disneyland. I quite like Americans. If we go back, I'll come visit you." Anytime kid . . . anytime.

TOKEN TIPS

Brian played very well on that trip because of his chipping. He had been working hard on it at our home course, and I'll let him tell you one of his tips. It's about how to have smooth tempo during a chip. If you've ever hit a chip that zipped over the green or you chunked the ground with your club, chances are you had poor tempo in your stroke. That being said, I'll hand my keyboard over to Brian and let him *type* you his tip. *Brian...*

"Thanks honey. It's so easy it's silly. If you have a two-syllable name, use that, if not, use the words, "one, two.' I use my name, 'Brian.' On the back stroke of my chips, I say, '**Bri—**' and on the follow-through, I say '**an.**' This also works with the words, 'one, two.' What you want to achieve is a steady tempo with your chip. Most beginners tend to move back just fine, but the lack of confidence sets in fast and they either slow down or speed up during their follow-through. The tempos usually never match. By saying either your name or 'one, two' or anything else along those lines when you chip the ball, you'll do just fine."

TOKEN SIDE TIP If your name's Bob, the tip won't work.

BRIAN'S SIDE TIP If your game's in the toilet, this book should be too!

JIMMY KELLY

Who is Jimmy Kelly? He's just the greatest caddy in the world, that's all. Every fiber of him is as Scottish as the small town where he grew up and still lives. He's one of those guys you describe as a *character*—almost everything about him is over the top. I first met Jimmy on one of our now annual trips overseas to the birthplace of my two passions: my husband and my golf. It was 1990 and our sixth trip to Scotland in as many years. This week we'd spend our vacation at the Gleneagles Hotel in Perthshire, Scotland. It's a Scottish treasure, over eighty years old. They have three magnificent eighteen-hole courses, a nine-hole par 3 course, and a fabulous hotel.

Brian and I were on the putting green warming up—well, Brian was warming up, I was just trying to keep warm—when through the early fog Jimmy approached us. As for his physical specs, he's in his fifties but looks at least ten years older than that. His face is the road map of a hard life he looks like he's been

to hell and back. The scars and wrinkles he wears tell the stories of bar room brawls and golf wisdom. He's an old-school caddy. Retro. He smokes in his sleep, and for many a year he'd put a shot of anything in his black coffee. If I lived one day in his shoes, I'd be hooked up to life-support machines. But for Jimmy, it works just fine.

There wasn't much conversation on the first tee; Jimmy just took the driver out of my bag and handed it to me. I said to him, "I'd like to tee off with my 3-wood, I hit that better than my driver."

My friend Jimmy Kelly

"Nah, hit this lass, it's the right club."

"OK, driver it is."

After a shaky tee shot, two mediocre iron shots, one chip, and two putts later, Jimmy had finished his overall assessment of my golf game. Standing on the second fairway, Jimmy handed over the club he wanted me to hit. That's where I broke rule number one, again. In Jimmy's book, you don't question his golf club selection. This time I didn't even actually *say* anything to break rule number one. Jimmy handed me the club, and I looked at the bottom of it to see which iron he wanted me to hit. That's a no-no, and I was about to get my very first Jimmy Kelly golf lecture.

"Now dear, don't be looking at what club I gave you. I saw you play the first hole; I know what you need to hit; I know how far it is to the green; and I know how far you can hit a ball."

In Jimmy's book, you don't question his golf club selection.

"You were able to tell all that from just one hole with me?"

"I only needed half a hole."

I hit the club he gave me, and the shot landed right in the center of the green. He was spot on with the club and the yardage.

"Now promise me you won't look over any more clubs I give you." Right there he had me.

Jimmy's passions are smoking, drinking, gambling, tasteless jokes, and handing you the perfect club time after time. If you ask him what the time is or what the actual date is, you may have to look elsewhere. But one thing he's always 100 percent right about is giving you the exact yardage and the proper club. He has a God-given talent for it.

Jimmy loves to wager on the golf course. Big shock! It doesn't necessarily have to be about golf either—he'd bet on anything, bets that he could never possibly win.

"I bet that you can't go a full round without swearing" (number 4 on the Jimmy Kelly list of passions).

"I don't have to swear—I can f***ing control it if I want to. Oh, sorry . . ."

"We'll just see about that. Twenty pounds says that you can't last eighteen holes without saying one curse word."

"Are you f***ing mad, twenty pounds!"

"Oops. How about five pounds?"

"Five pounds? It's a f***ing bet! That last one doesn't count by the way."

He cracked after two holes. The foursome ahead was searching for all four of their drives in the woods. Slow golfers drive Jimmy batty. He paced back and forth across the tee box four or five times losing patience with each step. Finally he threw his hands up in the air and said just loud enough for Brian and me to hear, "You damn hackers, will you f***ing move it!" he turned back to us, reached into his pocket, handed over the five pounds and said, "Ahh, s**t, I knew I couldn't do it."

Jimmy and I have a special relationship. He knows my game and, just as important, he knows *me*. If I am not playing particularly well, Jimmy has the cure: his jokes. They are so bad, yet so good. Every great comedian has a distinct, unique sense of timing. They have a certain style to their delivery. When you watch the top comedians, you can usually tell when the punch line is coming. But what you can't guess is the punch line itself. Jimmy fits that mold perfectly. Part caddy, part comedian. Jimmy has

"It's been so long since me and the wife had sex that we can't remember which one's supposed to get tied up. Hit this."

his own special way of delivering his punch lines. He'll stand holding the club he wants you to hit, but doesn't give it to you until he delivers the punch line. This is a typical hole . . .

"Jimmy, there's a lot of wind coming at me, water to right, and the green is surrounded by bunkers? What's my shot?"

"It's been so long since me and the wife had sex that we can't remember which one's supposed to get tied up. Hit this." With that, he'd hand me the club he wanted me to hit.

"Jimmy, should I flop it on the green or chip and run?"

"My wife's so flat we had to get T-shirts printed up that said 'Front.' Chip and run. Hit this."

He knew that a few holes of his personal brand of comedy would cure any flaws my swing might be having on any given Sunday. And if those jokes didn't do the trick and my swing was meant to falter for eighteen holes, I just didn't care with Jimmy on the bag.

It was probably the third or fourth visit to Gleneagles when Jimmy said he was a fan of *Charlie's Angels.* But even that was delivered in classic Jimmy fashion. He said, "You know you're not the best golfer of the lot."

"What?"

"The best golfer of all the Angels is that Joy'slen Smith gal."

"Who?"

“Joy’slen. The looker. You know, the looker on the show. The brunette.”

“The best golfer of all the Angels is that Joy’slen Smith gal.”

“You mean Jaclyn Smith.”

“Yes, Joy’slen. She can really hit the ball, that beauty, she can hit it.”

Now I don’t even know if Jaclyn has ever held a golf club and neither did Jimmy, but he loved to wind me up.

On the next shot, I found my ball lying hopelessly in a bunker as big as my home state. One thing about Scotland’s golf courses—either the bunkers are tiny round holes of doom or they’re the size of South Dakota. It took more than a few swings to get the ball out on that hole. Jimmy looked on holding the rake, and when I finally hit it out he joined me in the bunker to clean up my mess. But not without offering his little remark: “The looker would have gotten out of here in one shot.” I laughed. *Inside.* It was funny, but I couldn’t let Jimmy know that. I marched up and down the entire length of the bunker leaving my footprints and kicking sand everywhere. He flipped out and said, “What in hell are you doing? I have to rake all that now!”

I walked over to where he was standing on the rim of the bunker and gave him a great big grin and said, “So, Joy’slen Smith is the looker, huh?” As I marched away I heard laughter and expletives for fifty yards.

I know this is going to sound strange, but Jimmy and I have a weird connection. It's amazing, but every time I'm in Scotland, whether it's at a tournament or on a golf vacation, Jimmy just shows up without me ever having to call ahead. No matter what course I'll be playing on, he knows it in advance. I call it C.S.P.: *Cheryl Sensory Perception.*

The last time I saw him was distinctly more special than any other time. I was going to play at Gleneagles in a tournament hosted by Scottish racecar champion, Jackie Stewart. It was the twenty-first time Jackie put on the event, which was a benefit for different charities across Scotland. It was a unique, Scottish-flavored tournament, featuring golf in the morning and a clay pigeon shooting contest in the afternoon. I wasn't nearly as excited about the clay pigeon shooting as I was about the golf. I told the tournament director on the phone to let Jimmy know that I would need him on the bag. Even though I knew Jimmy had C.S.P. and he would show up anyway, I wanted to make sure. Sometimes even telepathic wires get crossed.

I know this is going to sound strange, but Jimmy and I have a weird connection.

That's when the director hit me with horrible news. He said that Jimmy's caddying days might be over.

"What do you mean? What happened?"

He told me that over New Year's, Jimmy had been stabbed. My heart sunk. Jimmy is more than a friend, he's a golf friend. So when I heard that Jimmy had been hurt, I was horrified. I figured I'd never see him again in my life, that I had lost a good friend.

It was hard to imagine that Jimmy would not be on my bag when I arrived that spring. I knew I'd miss Jimmy, but I was going to play this tournament for him. I wanted to play well and do him justice.

> *I actually love this kind of pressure moment on the golf course.*

I walked out of the clubhouse after checking in and thought I was seeing a mirage. "Is that Jimmy standing there or am I losing it?"

He walked over and said, "You didn't think I was going to let you go it alone, did you?"

The only answer I could get out was one word, "JIMMY!" I was so excited to see him. I looked at him completely stunned and just kept yelling, "Jimmy, Jimmy, Jimmy, you're here!"

This was Jimmy's first day back on the course since he had been stabbed, and it was sure to be a memorable one. I was paired with tennis great Stan Smith. We were playing alongside another tennis star, Rod Laver, and his partner, Diana Ross's ex-husband, shipping magnate Arne Naess.

Jimmy and I were having a great tournament. He'd calculate the yardage, take out a club, and say, "You're a wonder of a wee

woman, hit this." We were in the zone all day. We reached the seventeenth green, a short par 4, and our team was one point behind the leaders, who just happened to be Rod and Arne. Stan and I had a quick talk about our strategy; if we could make some points on this hole then we'd have a chance to tie the leaders heading to the last. I swear to you, this conversation not only happened, but it was on the actual BBC television broadcast.

Stan said, "I'm going to drive the green and make my putt for eagle."

I answered him back with the same confidence, "I'll get on the green in two and make my putt for a natural birdie."

I was getting two strokes on that hole and if I could roll in the birdie, it would count as a one on my scorecard. Stan drove the green, *just as he said*, and made his putt, *just as he said*. I was on the green in two, *just as I said*, and feeling the pressure. The putt I was looking at was a little more than thirty feet. I actually love this kind of pressure moment on the golf course.

There was nothing else on my mind except, **make a birdie.**

There was nothing else on my mind except, *make a birdie.* Jimmy stalked all thirty feet between my ball and the cup. He wanted that birdie as badly as I did. He was reading the putt from every direction, and when *he* was ready, he gave me the line. He carefully showed the spot he wanted me to roll my ball over so it would catch the break and roll down to the cup. Now it was up to me. I lined up my ball, trusted Jimmy's read, trusted my stroke, and rolled in my birdie putt! And rolled in my birdie putt! Sorry, I just had to say it again. What a moment. Or should I say, miracle.

Rod and Arne both parred and we were now tied for the lead heading to the eighteenth hole. I teed off and hit a beauty. Center cut right down the middle of the fairway, perfect position to reach the green on my next shot.

In the middle of my practice routine for my approach shot to the green, Arne walked up behind me and whispered, "That's the sexiest swing I've ever seen." Mind you, this billionaire has said maybe a handful of words to me all day, and now he's decided to come up and offer me this little tidbit. That my swing is the *sexiest* he had ever seen? I let my token chick guard down for a nanosecond and got out of the mind-set for hitting my next shot. Arne had actually *gamed* me out of the confident swing I'd had all day. He threw me with his remark and psyched me out of hitting a good shot. I hit my approach shot short and wound up making bogey on the hole. Stan and Rod both made par so it was down to Arne. Arne rolled in his birdie putt, and they beat us by one stroke.

He had hit a great tee shot, a wonderful approach shot, and a confident birdie putt. He played the hole in textbook fashion. Everything was textbook except his remark to me. It wasn't sportsmanship; it was psychological warfare. I vowed that was the last time that I would ever let anyone get into my head during a golf tournament.

In the end, it didn't matter. What really mattered was that Jimmy was back. We talked about life and his new appreciation for it. He told me that after he had been stabbed, he spent weeks staring out of his hospital window wondering if he'd ever get out of there. He swore that if he did, he'd have a fresh outlook on everything. Maybe even cut down a little on the cursing. I remember that afternoon was the best we ever shared.

When the afternoon was over and we said our

I let my token chick guard down for a nanosecond and got out of the mind-set for hitting my next shot.

good-byes, we both had tears in our eyes. He wiped his eyes and blew his nose and said, "You know I've caddied for f***ing princes! But you're special, you're a friend." So are you, Jimmy. So are you. He's rarer than a hole in one that Jimmy Kelly. I've learned so much from him. Not only about golf, but about life. I can honestly say I love the guy.

"You know I've caddied for f***ing princes! But you're special, you're a friend."

TOKEN TIPS

With Jimmy caddying for me, one thing I didn't have to worry about was course management. Course management is when you put a realistic thought into what shot you're going to hit. Here's an example: say you sliced your drive and wound up missing the fairway to the right. You can see the green in front of you, but there are trees and a bunker in your way. Instead of going for it and hoping to pull off a miracle shot, you play safe and smart by hitting your ball *away* from the trouble and getting it back on the fairway. This way you at least have a chance of getting your next shot on the green. Once there you can make one putt and save your par or two putts for a bogey at worst. Poor course management only leads to double, triple, and quadruple bogeys. TOKEN UPDATE: I spoke to Jimmy around Christmas time, and he told me he was sober and going to meetings. What a great gift! Yay, Jimmy!

TOKEN SIDE TIP If you can make your family breakfast, pack school lunches, walk the dog, and still make your 9:30 A.M. Pilates class, than having good course management should be a breeze.

IT'S A THIN LINE BETWEEN GOLF AND DEATH

My golf trips always seem to end up being about much more than a few rounds of golf. They're adventures in life. And 99.9 percent of the time they're both interesting and fun. This story is about the remaining tenth. The tenth that sneaks up out of nowhere and scares you more than a case of the yips. (*Having a case of the yips means that you've lost all mental confidence in your putting without warning. Caution: If you get the yips, seek immediate help from a professional. They can remove the yips before serious damage to your golf psyche occurs.*)

Now, for this year's trip to Scotland, Brian and I decided to go with something new and adventurous. A golf cruise. After booking the trip, we only thought about it being *something new*, it wasn't till after we started out that we realized it had become *something adventurous*. And after that, well, read on . . .

Our vessel was a magnificent 180-foot restored masterpiece. Elegant brass lamps, mahogany furniture, crystal glassware, the

My expression says it all. I am my own worst critic.

finest china, everything was very posh. It was like a golf time machine. It would take us to play at hundred-year-old golf courses along the west coast of Scotland. A few of the courses were on islands so remote that they were only accessible by boat. Our first stop would be to the Machrihanish Golf Club. It's located on the southern tip of The Mull of Kintyre between the Isle of Arran and the Hebrides. The first hole actually requires your drive to cross a corner of the Atlantic Ocean.

The twenty passengers onboard included golf journalists, golf travel executives, golf-related business types, and of course, just plain ol' golf folks, that being Brian and myself. Also with us for her maiden voyage was the proud owner of the boat.

After we set sail, there was a social mixer where no matter which conversation you eavesdropped on, it was about golf. Golf

jokes, memorable rounds, holes in one, the best courses, and so on. Minutes into the party a huge roar from the bright blue sky silenced us. The usual Scottish golf party crasher, known as inclement weather, had surfaced. In just minutes after the first boom of thunder, the sky went from bright blue to gray to pitch black. Severe gusting winds appeared, and the once calm ocean was now violently rocking. Our boat was being tossed as if it were on a trampoline. Liquor bottles were crashing off the shelves; furniture was being flung around the salon.

Normally, I never get sea sick, but there's a first for everything. My stomach was rolling, and I went back to the cabin to ride out the storm in my bed. Lying in the bed, I could feel what the captain was doing to battle the storm. He'd gun the engine hard, and ride up the face of a huge wave, then cut the throttle back when we reached the top. Then he'd whip the tail of the boat around and *surf* us down the wave. If he hadn't been able to maneuver the back of the boat, we'd have flipped over, capsized, end of story. In my bed, I could hear the engines rumbling—*ggggrrrr*—as the boat struggled to climb the waves. So much for lying in bed.

The usual Scottish golf party crasher, known as inclement weather, had surfaced.

I decided to go back up top to see what was happening. Quiet pandemonium was going on. No one was panicking, but the expression on everyone's face was the same: "Is this it?"

Brian and I never faced anything as severe as this, so we did the only thing you can do in that situation: pray.

All of the passengers were on deck except for one man. His brother came up to me and said, "This is no good. I can't get my brother out of the room. We all need to be up here together and he's lying in bed wearing his life jacket screaming, 'We're gonna die! We're gonna die!' He's always been a bit of a drama queen." We all laughed nervously at that remark, grateful for the smallest bit of humor. I know a few of us thought the life jacket idea was sounding pretty good.

Brian and I never faced anything as severe as this, so we did the only thing you can do in that situation: pray. We even started singing hymns, and everyone quickly joined in. Though we sang with gusto, we could not best the howling wind and the sound of the water crashing over the entire boat.

After about fifty minutes of doom, our prayers were answered. The storm passed, and the sea was calm once again. The black sky gave way to perfect blue as soon as the last raindrop had fallen.

The passengers were still in a daze, but my heart was breaking for the owner. He sat across from me, on a broken chair, surveying the terrible damage done to his beautiful ship with tears in his eyes. I couldn't even begin to imagine what he was going through.

The captain came out and you could see the storm had put a quick ten years on him. Once he saw that we were all in one piece, he told us he'd heard about the bad weather after we left port but our best chance was to continue on to our destination and try to outrun the worst of it. After he settled everyone's nerves, I was beginning to think that maybe, as a group, we overreacted a bit. But once I heard the next sentence, I thought maybe we didn't react enough. The captain told us in all his years at sea it was the worst *hurricane* he'd ever gone up against. A hurricane!

The passengers were still in a daze, but my heart was breaking for the owner.

Shortly after this trip, the movie *Titanic* was released. I didn't care for it.

TOKEN TIPS

Whether you're on a golf cruise or in the middle of your round, you can't stop Mother Nature. So if you have a tee time booked and it looks like there's a chance of rain, pack some rain gear in your golf bag. Every golf store has lightweight rain tops and pants that you can slip on right over what you're wearing. I also recommend that when you buy golf shoes, you get a pair that are waterproof. Most golf shoes are, but just double check before you buy them. Even if you're playing and it's not raining, the golf course can be wet. Especially during early morning rounds when the grass is moist from dew. So waterproof shoes are a must.

TOKEN SIDE TIP If you play frequently I recommend that you have two pairs of golf shoes. One sneaker type and one that's more of a shoe style. One day you may be playing at your local municipal course and you want the sneaker style, while over the weekend you may be playing at a resort and favor the shoe style. Let's face it token chicks, when it comes to shoes, we can never have enough.

P.S. If it's raining and the sky is flashing, throw those lightning rods (**your clubs**) into your bag and head for the clubhouse. Being struck by lightning is not the way you want to light up the course.

This was the wildest hole I've ever played. It happened in 2002 at the Monte Carlo Invitational. It's the final hole, and it's part of the opening ceremonies the night before. It's a seventy-five-yard par 3 that requires you to hit over a massive fountain and land on a green that sits at the entrance to the famed Monte Carlo Place du Casino. It was not only the first time I teed off in the middle of a bustling town square; it was also the first time I ever teed off in heels!

BBB:

BOYS BEHAVING BADLY

I call this chapter "Boys Behaving Badly" because that's what happens with some men. They can act like boys who are trapped in the body of a grown man. They revert back to their days in public school when they would punch a girl in the arm instead of telling her about a secret crush. Women know that some men struggle with manners. I'm not talking about forgetting to open a car door or pull out a chair—I'm referring to poor sportsmanship. Check that—poor sports*men*ship. Look, I'm not some great athlete or anything, but I do love to compete. And every now and then I come out with a win.

Boys and men who are BBBs all have the same reaction when a woman beats them at a sport: lots of muttering and kicking at the ground. I love to make a man mutter and kick.

You can tell straightaway when you've got a first-class BBB on your hands. Listen for the muttering. It's a dead giveaway. After you introduce yourself on the first tee, if you see his lips moving when he's standing alone, you may have a BBB in your foursome.

I was so excited my first year in the male-celeb-dominated pro-am world, and I was very much hoping to gain their acceptance. A few of them—Robert Wagner, Andy Garcia, Clint Eastwood, Jimmy Connors—accepted me without judgment. They may not have announced it in the locker room, but they were on my side. Some others would take a little work.

I accepted the fact I was getting invited to play in these events *because* I was a woman. That's cool. I knew that I could turn things around. In life it's not how you get the opportunity, it's what you make of it. I used this theory to break into the boys' club. I'd have to beat them at their own game.

One of my first chances came at Merv Griffin's resort in Paradise Island in the Bahamas. I was paired with a very famous older actor whose career I greatly respected—Burt Lancaster. A living legend—I was a big fan. I was eager to play a round of golf with him. When we were young girls, we all had crushes on Burt Lancaster. If you're a woman and you've seen the movie *From Here to Eternity*, then your idea of romance has to include making out in the surf.

I couldn't wait to golf with Burt and talk to him about some of the great films he starred in. I was so hoping he would share stories about his early days in Hollywood. I walked out of the clubhouse and saw him standing with a few of the other celebrities. The years of his movie-idol fame were behind him, but you could still see that rugged, masculine look that made him so sexy in his day. I walked over to introduce myself.

He looked me over, not in a good way, and mumbled to himself, just loud enough for me to hear, "Well, this is going to be a miserable day."

"Hi Burt, it's so great to meet you. I'm Cheryl Ladd, your pro-am partner today." He looked me over, not in a good way, and mumbled to himself, just loud enough for me to hear, "Well, this is going to be a miserable day." This man who used to make my heart throb as a teen was doing it all over again, making my heart throb. Only now it was throbbing for a different reason. He was making it very clear to me and everyone else that he was not happy to be playing with a woman. I was so torn. This was the fabulous Burt Lancaster, but what was with the attitude? Half of me wanted to wrap my arms around him, and the other half of me wanted to kick his ass at golf!

Good golfers thrive on energy. It gets our blood flowing. I took the negative energy he was shooting at me and channeled it into my own positive energy.

I had one mission, and that was to beat his crusty old butt silly.

Everyone in our group was having a blast. We were all playing well except you-know-who. We didn't talk at all, but I kept smiling in his direction. *Kill them with kindness, I say.*

I thought humor might melt his heart.

The first four holes we played as opposites. I was hitting every fairway, and he was missing every one. Either he missed it to the right or to the left. They call it "army golf," meaning, *left, right, left, right.*

My game was really grooving, and the other men in my group couldn't have been more complimentary. The more compliments they gave, the worse it got for Burt. My swing was clicking, while his swing was clonking. I actually began to feel bad for him. He was really putting so much additional unnecessary pressure on himself.

We got to the fifth green and still no communication between us. It was becoming a little ridiculous. I thought about ways to break the ice with him. I thought humor might melt his heart. It's supposed to be the universal language, right? I gave it a shot . . .

"Hey, Burt, have you ever heard the joke about the golfer and his wife who can't get a tee time?"

"Yes, I have."

Well, that didn't work. I guess it's on to plan B. I'm just going to have to beat him at his own game. It could have easily been a scene from his famous Western, *Gunfight at the O.K. Corral.* We were standing in the tee box at the next hole, staring each other down. On this par 3 tee box, he was going to reprise his role as

Wyatt Earp, and I'd be one of the Clantons. Well, one of their sisters at least. Burt and I were going to have a good old-fashioned duel. The modern way. We wouldn't use six-guns; our weapons would be 7-irons. That was the feeling I had. We'd pull out our clubs, take ten paces, turn around, and tee off!

Burt went first and hit a good shot. He landed about twelve feet from the cup, but you would have thought his ball had landed *in* the cup. It was the first time he connected all day, and he needed to celebrate. I finally teed up my ball. I needed the right swing thought—professional golfers always give themselves a good swing thought. Aha! Lightbulb moment, I'm an actor; I should act like a professional golfer. OK, good swing thought. My tee shot landed well inside his ball. He would be giving me an excellent read on my putt, which I knew would really bother him.

After my ball landed, I turned to Burt. He'd have to communicate now. I had just stuck my ball five feet from the flag—it's an unwritten golf rule that a "good shot" comment is absolutely, positively expected. I waited . . . and waited a little more. The other guys in our group had already thrown out their "nice shot" compliments; when was he going to speak up already? Never.

He stared at the green in shock.

I looked over to him and said, "It's going to be a nice day out here, huh, Burt?"

Another moment passed, then finally it was as if the sun came out from behind the dark clouds, and he said to me, "You know, it is going to be a nice day out here. That was a great shot, Cheryl."

Once again he became the fabulous Burt Lancaster right there on the sixth tee, and the rest of the day was amazing. He now accepted me, and I was a fan of his again. The rest of the round he became the best pro-am partner I'd had.

"Cheryl, what club are you going to hit here?"

"Cheryl, what do you think about my putt? Does it break left or right?"

"Cheryl, your husband is one lucky guy."

One nice golf shot took that male ego he'd carried around for years and left it sitting back on the tee box at that par 3 sixth hole. For good.

I think we can all agree that every golf match has its own story. Brian and I were in Maui for a tournament when we were paired with a world-famous Olympic athlete. Everyone knows him. He's as American as apple pie, but that's all I'm saying.

At the practice putting green, Brian and I introduced ourselves to the BBB, and he answered back with, "Nice to meet you. What are your handicaps?"

OK, I guess he wants to cut right to the chase.

"I'm an eighteen handicap and my husband plays to a twelve."

"Well, my handicap teeters between two and three."

He looked at us like he wanted congratulations about his low handicap. "Right now, it's more of a two."

"Wow, good for you." I was impressed. Then again he is an Olympian.

He suggested a wager. "Why don't we play for ten bucks a person?"

"No problem."

We get to the first tee, and he just picks up right where he left off at the putting green. He was taking some practice swings when he says, and get a load of this, "You know, I intimidate some of the PGA pros that play with me. I just hit the ball so far."

Tied. His BBB blood was boiling, and I was waiting for his head to explode.

Brian and I both rolled our eyes at that one.

The opening nine holes were a delight. For the token chick that is, not the BBB. After nine holes, using our handicaps (two vs. eighteen), we were tied! Olympic star against a woman who stands a little over five feet, three inches.

Tied. His BBB blood was boiling, and I was waiting for his head to explode. It was that painful for him. I think that when he told us he was either a two or a three, he hadn't been talking about his handicap, he had been talking about the age he acts on the golf course. He would cheer if my putts missed and wave his arms in excitement when I hit into the rough. What a son of a BBB he was!

Along with his *sparkling* personality, he practically whipped out the rulebook at every hole to make sure we were following the rules at all times. I will say that at every hole, he drove the ball past the rest of our group. But I guess that length off the tee sapped his golf etiquette. There is something in golf called "your honor"; it means that whoever has the lowest score on the previous hole tees off first. Even if the BBB didn't win a hole, he would always be the first to tee off. Which, the last time I checked, was against proper golf etiquette. What's next with this BBB? Is he going to use one of his gold medals to mark his ball on the putting green?

On the eighth hole, I missed the fairway with my tee shot and was in a bit of trouble. My ball had landed in the one spot on the course where it looked like there'd be no recovery. To borrow a classic golf phrase, I was in jail with no chance of parole. The BBB needed to remind me that my shot wound up in a bad spot.

"What a shame. Do you want to take a penalty drop?"

"No thank you. I see an opening in the tree ahead. I'll just punch my shot out back onto the fairway. No drop needed."

"I'd take the drop if I were you—you'll never get that shot out of there."

You'd have been proud of me. I just smiled and proceeded to set up my shot.

The BBB needed to remind me that my shot wound up in a bad spot.

There was one small fork in the tree ahead. If I could hit a low punch shot and thread my ball through it, I'd land on the fairway in decent shape. I had that ball in the back of my stance, weight forward, ready to hit the best punch shot of my life. I took a half-swing back and punched that ball right between the tree limbs. Perfect shot. As my ball was sailing cleanly between the limbs of the tree, the BBB was yelling, "*Noooooo.*" The negativity coming from him was truly shocking. Why? Because this person makes a great living today as a motivational speaker! How's that for icing on the cake? He gets paid big bucks to give lectures on being positive in all aspects of life. Except on the golf course, I assume.

As my ball was sailing cleanly between the limbs of the tree, the BBB was yelling, "Noooooo."

That afternoon, my clubs were doing all my motivational speaking for me.

The best is yet to come. After the first nine holes are done and we're tied, he proposes a new bet. I'm all ears BBB, lay it on me.

"Next nine holes, double or nothing, no handicap!"

What? He's a two handicap, I'm an eighteen, and now he's challenging me to double the bet and play without giving me any strokes? You're on!

It looks like our gold-medal winner has hit the wrong ball. So sad.

We stayed tied all the way to the eighteenth tee.

After we all teed off, the BBB gets in his cart and starts racing to his ball. He's so angry we're tied that he must hit his ball immediately. Even if he is going to hit out of turn—again. No matter though. He gets to the ball that was the longest of all the drives and hits it onto the green. Brian, meanwhile, was standing over a ball on the fairway and asked the BBB probably one of the worst questions you can ask in competitive golf.

"Excuse me, what ball are you playing?"

Oh no. The BBB had committed the cardinal sin. He hit the *wrong* golf ball. He didn't answer, so Brian asked him again.

"What ball are you playing?"

With some definite hesitation, the BBB answered in a tone now crackling with fear.

"Titleist 2," he muttered. (Remember, I love making them mutter . . .)

Brian soaked in his answer and then hit him with this doozy, "Really, Titleist 2, huh? Cheryl, what ball are you playing?"

"Titleist 3."

It looks like our gold-medal winner has hit the wrong ball.

So sad. For him! Brian looked at the ball sitting at his feet, it was the BBB's.

"It would appear that you hit my wife's ball, which we all know is against the rules. The penalty being that you forfeit the hole. Since this *is* the last hole and you've broken the rules blatantly and you both were tied, you lose!"

He flipped. I saw steam coming out of his nose as he asked, "You're not gonna pull that rules crap on me!"

Huh? He'd been holding his rulebook at every hole all afternoon, and now he was left just holding his BBB.

Brian is my shining knight time after time.

We finished the hole and drove our carts back to the clubhouse, where he grabbed his golf bag and announced, "I'm leaving."

Good. I then asked him, "Hey, what about the twenty bucks?"

"What about it?"

"Can I have it?"

"No."

What? No? He refused to pay. Refused! Just looked at me and said, "*No.*" I'm sure he wouldn't try that at a casino in Las Vegas.

But it's all good; the pro-am golf world is a small one. I knew our paths would cross again and that I'd collect my twenty bucks plus interest and a small late-payment fee. Two years later Brian and I just happened to be in the same event with guess who? It gets even better: Brian was actually going to be on his team! I don't think the BBB recognized Brian right away as the man married to the token chick on whose bet he had welched. On the first tee, he went into his patented speech.

Listen guys, some of you can act like children sometimes.

"What's everyone's handicap? I hit it far . . . Don't be intimidated . . . Who wants to bet!"

Brian is my shining knight time after time. Right after the BBB finished his routine spiel, Brian said, "I'm sorry—I can't bet with you. You don't pay up when you lose."

Brian looked him in the eye and saw the penny drop. He also knew what Brian was about to say next, and there was nothing he could do about it.

"This man still owes my wife twenty dollars from the last time we played with him."

Silence fell over the group. The other partners looked at the BBB with grins on their faces, "You lost to his *wife*, huh?" Ouch. Can someone please get an ice bag at the first tee for the BBB with the severely bruised ego?

In perfect BBB timing, he pulled a twenty-dollar bill out of his pocket and handed it over. Brian nodded and said,

"Thanks, now we can play. I'll make sure my *wife* gets this."

The reality is that the BBB could have easily won that day if he had just relaxed and had some fun. But it was *sooooo* important for him to win; he put way too much pressure on himself. He really needed to do some motivational muttering to himself—maybe that would have helped.

Allow me to do a little motivational speaking on my own. Listen guys, some of you can act like children sometimes. If you're a BBB, it's not too late or too hard for you to turn around and be a BBN. A boy behaving nicely. Speaking for the girls, we'd all like you much better if you did. And girls, if the men can't understand how to make the transformation, give them a dose of what they know best. Drive them to a school yard and punch them in the arm.

TOKEN TIPS

Being a good golfer requires knowing how to hit different types of shots. The everyday expression is, "The more shots in your bag, the better." The token chick expression is, "The more shoes in your closet, the better."

When I was playing against the Olympic BBB, I needed a *punch shot* in order to get my ball back on the fairway. My teacher, John Hardy, showed me how to hit that punch shot. This is a shot all of us token chicks need to learn. Especially in the beginning when you miss a lot of fairways and need to get the ball back in play.

1

Place the ball in the back of your stance . . .

2

. . . and keep your weight forward. Swing the club halfway back so your left arm is at nine o'clock.

TOKEN SIDE TIP I've demonstrated these tips for a right-handed golfer. If you play lefty, hold the book up to a mirror and read it that way. OK, just reverse everything if you're a lefty.

My teacher also professes that great balance is key to having a great swing. Proper balance allowed me to hit that sweet shot on the par 3 with the BBB standing right next to me. The best way to accomplish this is by *holding the finish position at the end of your swing.* If you're able to hold your finish naturally and not fall to one side or move forward after you've hit the ball, it means that you've transferred your weight properly. You achieved smooth balance during your swing. An easy way to hold your finish is to envision being in a picture on the cover of a golf magazine. Trying to copy that nice finish pose professional golfers have. That's the same finish you want to have.

3

On the follow-through, make sure not to go all the way around to a full finish. Finish at halfway just like in your backswing. You can do this shot with two different finishes and accomplish two different goals. If you need to hit a punch that will fly and land softly, play the ball in the middle of your stance and keep the club pointing up on your follow-through.

4

If you want the ball to run (in other words, you need it to keep rolling after you've hit it), position the ball in the back of your stance and make your finish look like this. My club is literally **pointing** at my intended target. This finish position keeps the ball moving low above the ground. This is a great shot when you have to hit it under trees or against the wind.

TOKEN CHICK MOMENTS

Token chick moments are those where we thrive. More than likely, against the odds.

You only need three ingredients to make a great token chick moment. A tablespoon of yourself, a heaping portion of your accomplishments, and of course, a dash of the opposite sex. One of the great joys of show business is the variety of opportunities that present themselves. Two of my top token chick moments came through the help of the NFL. Yes, *that* NFL. The one that kidnaps our husbands and boyfriends every Sunday afternoon and Monday night from September through January. The first one happened when I sang the national anthem at Super Bowl 14. Oops. Sorry guys, I meant Super Bowl XIV. Speaking of which, can someone please explain the Roman numeral thing to me when it comes to the Super Bowl? How come you don't use it all season long for the wins and losses record? "The Rams had a good year, they're XI and V."

Before I go into the story, I bet a lot of you don't know that I sing.

Before I go into the story, I bet a lot of you don't know that I sing. My singing career came about as unexpectedly in my life as playing golf. When I was a kid, my dad would get together with some of his buddies on weekends, and they had country music jam sessions while all the kids played outside. Often I found myself leaving the games of tag and watching the band instead. I'd be dancing, tapping my toes, and feeling the music, when one evening my father asked me if I wanted to join in and sing with the band. I was eight years old, and my favorite country song was "Cotton Fields." I sang it with them that night, and music grew to be a big part of my life. Years later, I joined a local group called the Music Shop Band. We were the ultimate bar band. We'd play any type of music you could hear on a jukebox. Country, jazz, rock, pop, opera. *All right, not opera.* Whatever song the people in the bar wanted to hear, we'd do it. That band was my ticket out of South Dakota. We decided to go on the road and head to California. Ever since I was a little girl, I wanted to be an actress, and this would be my chance to get there and realize my dream. I remember my mom crying for three days before I left, but my dad really put her at ease about it. I was only seventeen years old then; naturally my mother was a bit concerned about me heading to California and trying to break into what she called the "big bad wolf of show business." My dad told her,

"She's been telling us that this is what she wants to do with her life since she was three or four years old. If we don't let her go, we'll lose her forever. We have to trust that we did a good job raising her and let her become who she is." My dad was the best.

With my high school diploma in one hand and a suitcase in the other, I was on my way to California. We performed at different bars along the way to Los Angeles, and as my luck would have it, we broke up. But I wasn't about to go back home just yet. A short time later I got my first real job in Hollywood as the singing voice of Melody on the cartoon *Josie and the Pussycats.* I eventually went on to record three albums. I did pretty well in the music world—here in the U.S., I had a top-forty single and I was the number one recording artist in Japan. Now that you have the inside skinny on my singing career, let me get back to where I was . . . *the Super Bowl.*

That year, the big game was to take place at the Rose Bowl in Pasadena, and it just so happened one of the teams competing for the title was the local team—the Los Angeles Rams. Every seat was filled with either diehard football fans or someone who worked in show business. Definitely high pressure. It wasn't the football fans that I felt the pressure from, it was the Hollywood crowd. They're the harshest critics anywhere. They may be applauding during your performance, but it's all about surviving the next day. When the phone calls are made . . . "I went to the Super Bowl yesterday. Yeah, great game, but what about that national anthem, huh? I know, I know. Well, it's a tough song for anyone." There was no way I'd let that happen.

Some years later, I was on Broadway starring in *Annie Get Your Gun*. Before each show I closed my eyes and *thought* about the performance I was about to give. Even though it was the same show every night, to me, each one had to be better than the night before. Whether I was performing on Broadway or playing golf, I always want to do better than the time before. Before the house lights dropped and another show began, the cast would mill about backstage with nervous energy. I had it too. But I closed my eyes and breathed deeply, and got into my zone, clearing away my nervous energy. I waited for the stage manager to whisper those famous words in my ear, "five minutes," then hit the stage ready to rock and roll.

I didn't have that ritual in place on Super Bowl Sunday. The nervousness I was feeling had turned the butterflies in my stomach into hummingbirds. I was tapped on the shoulder by the pregame show coordinator, who said, "We're ready for you now."

I started walking out of the tunnel and saw a never-ending sea of people. Talk about tunnel vision. This one scares the daylights out of you. I felt like a Roman gladiator entering an arena for a fight to the death.

On the golf course, a good swing thought would do the trick to calm my nerves, so here I needed a good *sing* thought. I looked at my watch and thought, "In a few minutes this whole thing will be over, enjoy it while it lasts." It worked. I embraced what was about to happen; I walked out of the tunnel, cool, calm, and collected. I was ready. As a matter of fact, I was so calm I even let my mind wander for an instant. I walked onto the playing field and looked at the gorgeous lush grass and thought for a split second, "Who's their gardener? My lawn never looks this good."

In order to reach the center of the field where I'd be singing, I had to walk along the visiting team's bench. That team was the notorious Pittsburgh Steelers. They were called the "steel curtain" back then and were the most dominant team in Super Bowl history. In six years, they appeared four times and won every time. However, this Super Bowl would be the end of their dynasty. Walking by the Steelers was like walking through a redwood forest. Football players are so huge in everyday street clothes, but when you put them in shoulder pads and helmets and their uniforms, they look like giant warriors from the future.

On the golf course, a good swing thought would do the trick to calm my nerves, so here I needed a good sing thought.

I heard them announce my name on the PA system, and it reverberated throughout the stadium. To me, it sounded like my name was bouncing off every fan's chest in slow motion.

While I stood there looking at the fans, I swear I could see the pupils of their eyes. My whole body began to vibrate like I had just been plugged into an electrical outlet. That's what the fans' energy felt like to me. Electricity in my veins. I was ready. I was confident. Let's get on with it! Start the music! *Not quite yet . . .*

You've got the picture—minutes till game time, cheering fans, the anthem about to start, what comes next? The biggest American flag I have ever seen gets unfurled across the entire field. Next come the fighter jets passing overhead while military officers in full dress salute and march onto the field.

It's the same as having a solid preshot routine in your golf game: you block out the distractions and focus on the job at hand.

I started to lose it emotionally. I stood there thinking about how proud I was to be an American and what that meant to me. The entire crowd was caught up in the moment as one. The cheers, the fireworks, the jets flying overhead, and the flag waving were bringing me to the brink of tears. I hadn't anticipated this part. I had factored in the nerves, but I hadn't anticipated the rush of emotion. I needed to hold it together. Tears, even though they were tears of pride, weren't going to work at this particular moment. Besides, I don't think any of the players were carrying tissues.

The music started, and I quickly pulled myself together to sing. My focus was not forgetting the words. That was my mission. It's the same as having a solid preshot routine in your golf game: you block out the distractions and focus on the job at hand.

TOKEN SIDE TIP
Since our guys are glued to the couch during Super Bowl Sunday, make it Token Chick Sunday. If you live in a warm climate, gather all the girls and hit the golf course, or, if you live where it's cold, gather all the girls and hit the stores! By the way, the latter works in a warm climate as well.

If you trust your muscle memory, you're good to go. The last thing in the world I wanted was to wind up on a sports bloopers show in a montage of singers who forgot the words while performing our national anthem. I began to sing.

"O, say can you see . . ." After I got the first few words out, I was on autopilot. Cruise control. Home free. Singing the anthem happened so fast that it was over before I even realized it. I did it without flubbing any words or hitting any notes that make animals howl.

It was a proud and privileged feeling.

As I was walking off the field, I had to go past the Steelers' bench again, only now it was less than five minutes later and I felt like a completely different person walking by them. I was about to step into the tunnel where my incredible journey began when the Steelers' superstar receiver, Lynn Swann, stopped me. He was minutes away from game time, trying to get into the zone for the Super Bowl, a game that defines careers, but he took a moment to tell me something. He hunched down. *Way* down. He smiled with that beautiful Lynn Swann smile, winked at me, and said, "You're not the right color to be singing that good, girlfriend." Now *I* was six feet tall.

Ten years later, I was playing in the NFL Golf Shootout in La Costa and saw some of the players from that Super Bowl. They

Cheryl and Terry Bradshaw

were retired now, but they were still bigger than life. The NFL Golf Shootout has football stars and celebrities playing to raise money to benefit different charities. The shootout isn't your average golf tournament. It's also a skills challenge. Allow me to explain. Besides playing in the tournament, everyone competes in six different golf challenges. Longest drive, medium-iron shot, get out of trouble shot, pitch shot, sand shot, and, of course, putting.

The one the fans were most excited about seeing was the long-drive contest and for obvious reasons. Since football players have at least four times the strength and twice the size of an average man, we were all expecting five-hundred-yard drives and nothing less. This was not going to be one of those days. No, no, no.

The longest-drive contest is without a doubt the hardest to win. Not only because of the length off the tee that's necessary, but because you also need a little luck. The longest drive is only contested on one particular hole. It's selected in advance and deemed "the long-drive hole." Not only that, you must hit your tee shot in the fairway in order for it to count.

The law of averages will tell you that hitting the sweet spot on the club, hitting the ball far, and hitting it in the fairway might be asking a little much.

The players in my group teed off and each tried to reach the moon. *Both cheeks.* That's what it's called in golf when you swing with all your might. I think you get my drift. I was next to go.

Standing on the tee at the long-drive hole was the most relaxed I'd felt all day. There was no pressure. I knew I wasn't going to win this contest against three-hundred-pound football players. I took a practice swing. Next, I thought about one of my favorite swing thoughts. It's the golfer's prayer, "Please, Lord, give me the strength to hit this ball easy." When we all want to bust a long drive, our first instinct—even for NFL players—is to swing really, *really* hard. Huge mistake. Swinging with a nice, steady tempo is the key to a long, straight drive. It assures pure contact with the clubface and keeps you in solid balance. I took another practice swing, quickly saying the prayer to myself, "*Pleaslrd ltme hitthsblesy.*" I teed up my ball and took one more practice swing.

Then WHACK! My ball soared straight down the fairway. It caught a tremendous bounce off a downhill slope and kept on going like the Energizer bunny.

To mark the spot on the fairway where the longest drive up to that point has reached, a small signboard is stuck in the ground where the ball landed. If your ball lands farther than the sign, you're the new leader. You write your name on the board and stick it back in the ground where your ball landed. Walking down the fairway, I saw the sign in the ground and something amazing. It was a gift from the golf gods. When I reached the sign, I saw that my ball was just past it. The guys in my group were in shock. I was in shock. Trembling, I wrote my name on the board as the new long-drive leader and stuck the sign back in the ground. Even though my drive was way out there, I didn't think it would last against the NFL players who still hadn't had their turn. It felt amazing to write my name on that board. Even if it was only going to be there for a short time—so I thought—the person that out-drives me was going to look at that board and see my name. That was enough of a victory for me.

At the end of most golf outings, there's a dinner for the participants. The amateurs, the pros, and the celebrities all hang out together and trade war stories from

The guys in my group were in shock. I was in shock.

They told me that I had won by a single inch!

their round that day. They use a few cocktails to either drown their sorrows from a bad round or toast their splendid play that afternoon. The prizes for all the winners are also presented at that dinner. I was at my table enjoying a cosmopolitan when they announced the winner for the long-drive contest. I heard it, but it didn't seem to be real.

"The winner of the long-drive contest is Cheryl Ladd."

Me? I looked down at my cosmo, "Did someone slip something in here, or did he just say that I won the long-drive contest?" Say that again?

"Cheryl, come up. You're the winner."

Here's the best part. When I was at the podium, they told me that I had won by a single inch! My shot had landed one inch farther than one of the NFL players' shots. While standing there looking around that room full of football players, all as stunned as I was, the thought of a pay-per-view event quickly crossed my mind: *Token Chick vs. the NFL in the Long-Drive Shootout.* Enough daydreaming. *What did I win?* They always have the best prizes at these events. I thought it might be a weekend at a golf resort or maybe a new set of golf clubs. I never would have expected the prize I won. But then again, the committee that makes up the list of prizes for the NFL shootout didn't expect the token chick to win the long-drive contest. They rightfully assumed that one of the football players would win that one. Hah! Never take a token

chick for granted! I know you're wondering what I won. It was a very *fitting* prize for an NFL player. So, just what do you give to the football player who has everything? An Armani suit, of course, in size 52 extra long! I held it up for all the players to see. When I walked back to my table, Marcus Allen, who's a really good golfer, laughed his head off and said, "How could you outdrive me? That should be *my* new suit!" But to this day, it's absolutely my favorite trophy.

TOKEN TIPS

At the driving range for that event, there was a golf instructor making the rounds to see if anyone wanted a mini lesson. *Yes, over here, please.* He gave me a tip on how to bust a long drive. It helped me win the long-drive contest and will add extra yards to your tee shots. When you take the driver back, make sure you have a big extension with your arms. Look at the pics, and I'll show you the differences between a poor extension and a proper one.

POOR EXTENSION

PROPER EXTENSION

When you have a poor extension, you're shortening your club's length, and you'll be robbing yourself of distance. You're turning a driver into the length of a 5-wood. Here's a good drill to maintain the proper amount of width. Place your driver headcover under your right arm.

When you make your shoulder turn, allow the headcover to naturally fall out when you get to the top of your swing. This easy drill keeps your arms from getting lazy at the top and keeps them working in your swing. Practice this ten thousand times a day and you're on your way! OK, just practice it for a few minutes and you'll still be on your way . . .

BREASTS

Breasts. Good, now that I have your attention, I'd like to talk about them. In golf, what separates the men from the women are mainly two things. Distance and breasts. Men hit the ball farther, and women have breasts. Other than that, if you can chip and putt, we're all equal out there.

On any golf course there are hazards and obstacles to deal with. Male golfers face water, sand, trees, et cetera. Female golfers face those same obstacles and more. Like having breasts and being pregnant. Maybe that's half true. I've seen a lot of men playing golf who look like they're at least fifteen months pregnant. We women constantly have to find ways to make our natural swing fit with our natural bodies. But our bodies are constantly changing in ways that men's bodies are not. What if it's that time of the month for us when our breasts are a little bigger than normal? It affects our regular swing. What if they're extra sensitive, so that even if dust fell on them it would sting? It affects our swing.

So, how can we make our breasts work for us in our golf swing?

. . . when I embrace them and get the sensation of feeling them a little against each arm, I'm in the perfect V.

Great question. I'm glad I asked it.

Here are two of the best breast tips you can get. (By the way, I challenge you to say that ten times fast.)

When a woman learns how to play golf and holds a club for the first time, she has to decide where the club sits around what God gave her. If you have small breasts, then you don't have to worry as much. You're blessed with a lot of freedom for upper-body motion. But if you have medium, large, or extra large breasts, hold the club and see how your arms react to your breasts. In other words, are you around them? Are you above them? Are you over them? Where are you?

I find that the best way to position your arms is to embrace your breasts. God gave them to you, and they should be embraced every chance you get. So for me, I find that when I embrace them and get the sensation of feeling them a little against each arm, I'm in the perfect V. When your arms hang down from your shoulders, the goal is to have them hang so they form a letter V. By embracing them, my arms aren't extended too far out, they're not too close in, they're just right. Also, embracing doesn't mean squeezing. This is golf, not a photo shoot. If you look down and see that you suddenly have extra cleavage, then your arms are too close together. Ease up a little so that you can breathe.

Here's breast tip number two. It's based on a classic swing tip: "Back to the target, chest to the target." That means when you've completed the backswing your back should be facing the target, and when you're in the finish position at the end of your swing, your chest should be facing the target.

Now let's take that same tip and *token chick-itize* it. "Back to the target, *breasts* to the target." Say it again: "Back to the target, *breasts* to the target." When you've reached your finish position you should be in a stance where you're showing the world your breasts. Your golf swing is a great excuse to show them off without having to do it intentionally. In your finish position, always try to have good, upright posture.

If you've got a club nearby, pick one up, or else just pretend you're holding one and try this drill. Swing the club and hold your normal finish position. Check your posture. Are you standing tall with your chest pumped out or are your shoulders slumped and you're slouching? Most likely you're slumping and slouching. Lift your shoulders a little and pump out that chest a bit, as if you're *proud* of your breasts. Swing the club again and this time focus on good posture and pumping out your chest when you finish. If you're doing it right, you may find that you're smiling suddenly. Why? Because you feel good, you've just swung the club well, *and* you have great breasts!

As for you men out there who may have, you know, a little breast action going, those tips will work for you too. Those and this one: lay off the carbs!

TOKEN TIPS

Since we're on the subject of golfing with something that women have—breasts—I want to continue with something women tend to do. Some of us sway during our putting stroke. Typically, this is very common when you first start playing. I actually discovered this tip during a late-afternoon round by myself. Some days when the sun sets, I like to walk a few holes by myself before dinner. It's a great ending to your day, it clears your mind, you're getting exercise, not to mention squeezing in some golf as well. Remember, playing golf doesn't mean that you need to get in a full eighteen holes for four and a half hours. You can walk out for nine holes or as many as you feel like playing. And don't worry that you'll be paying for eighteen holes and playing nine. All courses have different rates for both. They also have discounted rates in the afternoon, and the prices continue to go down as the day goes on. They're called twilight and super twilight rates. At a typical course in Southern California, you can play at five o'clock in the evening for around seven bucks. Not a bad deal. One more thing: playing a few holes doesn't mean that you need to carry every club and all the other junk that takes up space in your golf bag. Get a lightweight carry bag—they can weigh as little as two pounds and only take a max of eight clubs. In case you already have a lightweight bag lying around in

Fig. 1

your closet, I suggest that you buy a double carry strap from your local golf store (FIG. 1). They cost around twenty dollars and attach easily to any bag. It makes it much easier to carry your clubs, just like a knapsack.

OK, let me get to that tip about swaying during your putts. When I go out in the late afternoon, I'll let the setting sun analyze my swing. Here's how: when you can see your shadow on the course, take a moment to look at your swing in it. Shadows are like having a mirror on the course. I noticed in my shadow that during my putts I was swaying back and through with the putter motion. For putting, you want to have a solid foundation where the only moving parts are your shoulders.

FIG. 2

During the last few holes late one day, I was playing quickly so I could beat the sun before dark. To make things move faster, I left my golf bag on while I putted. I noticed that I holed more putts when I had my bag hanging from my back. Then I watched my putting stroke in my shadow, first with my bag on, then with my bag off. I saw that when I had the bag on, it acted like an anchor for my body (FIG. 2). That little bit of weight hanging off my back kept my balance centered and allowed me to move only my shoulders during my putt. The extra weight kept me from swaying back and kept me anchored throughout the putting motion. Try it the next time you're golfing and carrying your bag.

TOKEN SIDE TIP

Your golf bag should not be a replica of the everyday handbag you carry. You know, the one loaded with junk. Don't carry too much stuff in your walking bag. Six balls, a few tees, and maybe an energy bar. Also, make sure that you have comfortable golf shoes for the course. The newer styles available are as comfortable as your favorite pair of sneakers. And just as in our regular lives, token chicks, always make sure that your (golf) shoes match your (golf) bag.

GOLF + PMS =

THE PRE-MENSTRUAL SWING

When you're playing golf and you're PMSing, your emotions can sometimes cause you to explode. If he thinks you're a tad cranky during that time of the month in general, wait till he's standing there holding the flag while you have a downhill three-foot putt for a double bogey. Add in the frustration that he's probably told you it breaks right, when in fact you're sure it breaks left. No matter which way it breaks, for his sake, that putt had better drop. It's just plain hard to play well when you're PMSing. Your biorhythms are off, you have no coordination, and you want to dig up the man who invented the game just to yell at him. It can be rough.

Every woman hates PMS, but we love to golf. Combining the two culminates in the ultimate love/hate relationship. I classify golf PMS a little differently than the general one. It's the same emotional mood swings and occasional manic behavior you may get normally, only now, you're holding a weapon. Ahh, I mean a club. In other words, look out. When it comes to golf, PMS stands for the "Pre-Menstrual Swing." Because we really don't know what can happen next.

I'd rather battle Tiger Woods than raging hormones any day of the week.

PGA players interviewed on television after a win will say that the pressure coming down the stretch was so grueling and mentally exhausting that they can barely stand. Guys have it easy. Too easy! The nerve! I'd rather battle Tiger Woods than raging hormones any day of the week.

Think about an LPGA player in the same scenario and throw PMS into the mix. She's not only battling other players for the win, but also battling cramps, a headache, and a horribly bloated feeling. When an LPGA player wins a tournament while she has PMS, she should get *two* winner's checks and *two* trophies.

We don't give professional women golfers enough credit where it's due. I know that personally if I'm PMSing, probably like you, I want to be alone. I don't want to be followed down the fairway by a television crew, being interviewed about what club I'd just hit and how I'm feeling about the tournament. I want to be lying in bed under the covers waiting for my agony to end.

As a favor to the men out there, I'm going to give you the basic rules to follow if your playing partner is suffering from Pre-Menstrual Swing.

Rule №1:

Don't offer advice on how her putt breaks! Are you crazy or looking for a fight or both?!

Rule №2:

If she forgets to bring her putter to the green, make sure *you* don't.

Rule №3:

If she wants to hit *any* of your clubs, including your five-hundred-dollar driver that she might put a big skymark on, by all means, let her.

Rule №4:

If she hits one of your brand new five-dollar balls into the water, give her another one immediately without saying anything other than "you look beautiful."

Rule №5:

Just in case her Pre-Menstrual Swing gets completely out of control, make sure your golf bag is well stocked with chocolate. If she's doing badly on the course, break out a bag of M&Ms. If she's doing *really* badly, make it Peanut M&Ms.

TOKEN TIPS

When you're PMSing you can expect a loss of power. I know, even though you're raging inside, you are physically weaker. So I recommend using less of a swing and taking more club. The best way to get more distance with less effort and more consistency is by carrying a few fairway woods and hybrid clubs. They're easy to hit and offer excelled distance for swings that aren't packed with power.

TOKEN SIDE TIP
Up until a certain age, you have Pre-Menstrual Swing. You think that's tough? Well, buckle up baby, cause when you get a little older, you'll have the Pre-Menopausal Swing! YIKES!

This is one of my favorite shots to hit, and I bet it's not one of yours. It's my 3-wood off the fairway. It's one of the hardest shots to hit in golf. Especially when you have the scoreboard guy, a volunteer, and your caddy standing a few feet away. But I learned how to get over the fear of this shot. Mentally, since it was the weakest shot in my game, I was now determined to make it the strongest shot of my game. Most people try to hit this shot with too much power. This leads to either a fat shot or a chunked shot. Basically anything can happen—none of it good. Here's the approach you need to take. Look at my swing. If you weren't looking at the club I was hitting, you'd think I was hitting a relaxed ninety-yard wedge shot. That's the approach. Swing your 3-wood like it's a ninety-yard approach shot. You'll probably hit that 3-wood now about 180 yards. It's simple. If that swing gets me ninety yards with my 9-iron, then the same swing is going to get me 180 yards with my 3-wood. You're using the same swing, only a longer and bigger clubhead. Remember this phrase: **"Don't be a jerk, let the club do the work."**

CHARITIES

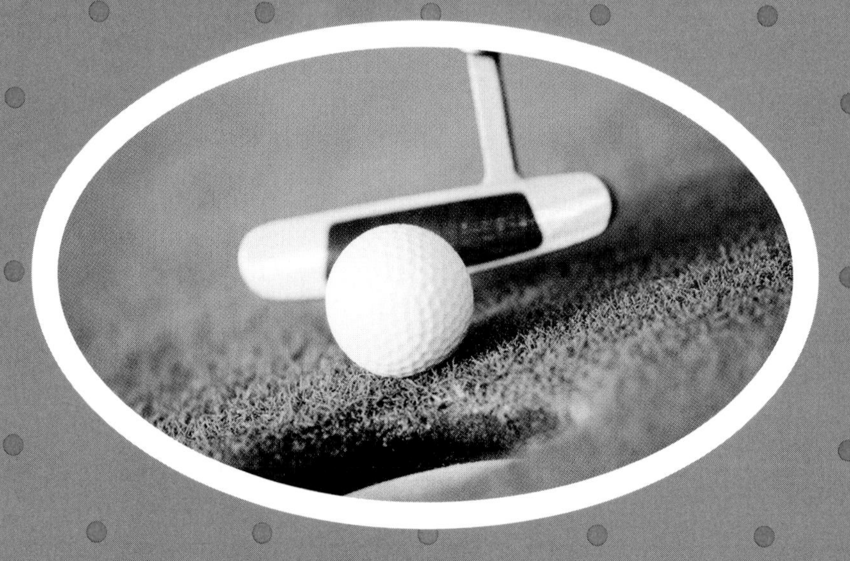

One of the great things about being a celebrity is the ability to raise awareness of the work that is done by charitable groups. An organization I've worked very closely with for many years is Childhelp USA. I've helped raise a lot of awareness for them and I hope a lot of donations. More on them later . . .

Obviously there aren't enough hours in the day to give your time to a charity, your family, and work. So like golf and life, balance is key. Sometimes when the moon and the stars are aligned properly, you can combine them all and succeed. I managed to pull this off, and the result was fantastic. I was approached by the LPGA about whether I would be interested in having my name on a pro-am tournament. So far, so good. There was an LPGA tournament in California, The Los Angeles Women's Championship that was in danger of losing its sponsors. It would be held at Oakmont Country Club in Glendale, California. After I agreed, I told the LPGA reps that I would help in every way I could to generate more public interest and get more sponsors to come onboard.

The first move I made was contacting my sponsor, Buick. They were in before I could even finish asking. With a big sponsor attached, I made the next call. Childhelp USA. I wanted them to be one of the charities that benefited from this tournament.

Excellent, everything's rolling smoothly. Ticket sales were booming and for the first time the tournament was shaping up to be huge.

I worked my tail off for this event and felt deep inside that there was only one thing I wanted in return for myself. That I pick who my playing partner is for the pro-am. *C'mon, that's fair . . .*

It was a no-brainer for me. I wanted to play with Annika Sorenstam. She was starting her rise then as one of the best female golfers ever.

At that time Annika was a young gun, or should I say a *gunness*, on the LPGA tour and was as good statistically as Tiger Woods. She had just celebrated her one-year wedding anniversary, and we talked about everything that afternoon, from playing golf to having a family. She asked me how I handle having a family and having to be away from them when I'm working out of town. I told her the most important part is to balance things and make time, not find time, but to make time, for the people that are most important to you. I connected to something else in her character, something that we both share. I truly feel incredibly fortunate to have my career. I've worked hard on it. Annika said that whenever she steps on a golf course she never forgets how fortunate she is to earn a living as a professional golfer. You can see it in her face. I think the best part of Annika's swing is when she makes contact with the ball. At the moment of impact one thing is always consistent. She's smiling. That's a woman who loves her job.

Annika and I before our round

Now I've played with Arnie and I've played with Jack. But the worst case of shaky nerves I ever experienced was when I played with Annika. As a golfer, I respect Arnie and Jack; no one can match their accomplishments. But as a *female* golfer, I was in *awe* of Annika. I wanted to play just like her, or at least hit one shot like she does! She's the prototype for the perfect golf swing, male or female. During our round, I had two personalities working. One was nervous, and the other was watching diligently how Annika approached the game. I used that once-in-a-lifetime proximity as a once-in-a-lifetime golf lesson. At each tee box, I would try to find new positions for myself to view her swing. Sometimes I would stand right behind her to watch how she set up to the ball, and then I'd watch from another angle during her shot from the fairway. When you're in that tee box breathing it with her you realize and you see the precision in her set-up and practice swings. When she hits the ball, it's as if you've seen a tightly choreographed graceful dance routine. The discipline that she shows in her routine is just that, discipline. Whether it was a two-foot putt or a twenty-foot putt, her routine was always the same. If all of us could apply that discipline and take a moment to line up every putt, I bet we'd shave an immediate five strokes off our games.

Fifteen thousand spectators had turned out the year before, and this year close to forty thousand attended. Those numbers would have been even higher if not for one small hitch in the plan. The tournament took place the second week of February. You know that song, "It Never Rains in Southern California"? It's a lie. It does rain. But it only rains for one month a year. I always felt the lyrics should have been, "It never rains in Southern California except in February." Saturday's round was a total washout, and the event was cut short from fifty-four holes to thirty-six. The winner was another good friend, Dale Eggeling, which made the week even sweeter.

Brian, Dale, and Cheryl

Although it almost didn't turn out that way. After completing her final round an hour earlier, Dale was in the clubhouse getting ready to leave. She was four shots off the lead and thought for sure that she was out of the running. Dale and her husband Mike were headed to Hawaii directly after the tournament, and Dale was itching to get out of Dodge, I mean, Glendale. It was getting late, and Dale was worried they would miss their flight. Mike said, "I don't think we should leave yet, the weather's turning and the players left on the course are starting to drop shots." Dale looked at the leaderboard and then up at the stormy clouds then over at Mike, who just said, "Get to the range and start warming up." Dale hit a few balls and the next thing she heard was "C'mon, there's a playoff." Dale didn't waste any time, after all, she still had a plane to catch. On the first playoff hole against Hiromi Koybashi, Dale sank a fifteen-foot birdie putt for the victory! Dale credits her win that year from having a new mental outlook. She worked hard on her

short game during the off-season, switched to a new set of clubs, and started the year with a positive, fresh attitude. One last note, someone thankfully finally spoke up about the most important aspect of the tournament. Move it to July and avoid the rain in February at all costs.

Now, I'd like to tell you a little about Childhelp USA and what they do. Their mission is simple. They deal with the physical, emotional, educational, and spiritual needs of abused and neglected children by focusing their efforts in the areas of treatment, prevention, and research. They believe that every child has a unique contribution to make to the world. They believe in unconditional love, which they feel is the foundation upon which all healing begins. Once their recovery is complete, the children are placed in good, loving foster homes. These children, who have seen the worst that life has to offer, deserve the best that can be provided while they're in the care of Childhelp USA, and they get it. OK, I know I've said enough, but do me a favor. The next time you're online doing nothing but surfing the net for your boyfriend from high school, check out their Web site, www.childhelpusa.org, and see what it's all about.

TOKEN TIPS

I watched Annika after the round while she practiced her putting. I liked her approach, and I try to do it myself. She puts eight balls in a circle around the hole about six feet away. Then she simply walks around and hits each putt into the hole in one stroke. The catch is, you miss one putt and you start over.

I think what amazed me the most is that we're pretty much the same size physically; she's a few inches taller than me, but when she hit her drives, wow! How does that small frame hit a ball 280 yards time after time? Well, I can't tell you. Not because I made some vow about divulging her secrets, it's just that I don't know how it happens. I asked her to tell me the key to her long drives and she said the two main factors were good tempo and not over-swinging. She said that women tend to swing back too far because they think a big windup leads to more distance. It only leads to poor contact and a loss of distance. Annika advises shortening your swing and maintaining the same tempo each time.

TOKEN SIDE TIP If an LPGA tournament passes through your town, take an afternoon and go watch it. Also, spend a little time at the driving range when the golfers warm up. They usually allow the spectators to sit in a grandstand and watch. Trust me, you may even pick up a tip or two.

HELL IN ONE

Not all of the stories in here are happy ones. After all, this is golf. I am hard-pressed to find anything else in life that can bring as much pain as it does enjoyment. Sometimes we can be playing so poorly that if someone suggested we stop for the day and go to a funeral, it would sound like fun.

I had been riding the golf high for some time. My game was at its best, which could only mean one thing. It was about to crash. For years, I had heard the horror stories from friends about their golf game going south, not only for the winter but for the rest of their lives. I always get sad when I see golf clubs rotting away in someone's garage because they have stopped playing. I bet for every person who says, "I play golf," there are a dozen who say, "I used to play golf."

Golf is a mental sport, and sometimes it gets the best of us. People told me that one day I would stop enjoying it, but I could not believe that day would ever come for me. After all, I am the token chick. Nothing short of kryptonite was going to stop me from loving it every time I stuck a tee in the ground. Nevertheless, that was then and this is now. Now just happened to come in the form of . . . Wait—let me collect myself for a second. It still leaves such a scar that I have to say it, or in this case, type it, very fast.

The Sun Microsystems Par 3 Challenge.

The Par 3 Challenge is an annual event that features players from the PGA, LPGA, and Champions Tour. To make it fun for the television audience, they throw a celebrity (to the wolves) in there as well. To make it even more exciting for the people watching at home, a player getting a hole in one wins a million bucks! Well, half a million. The other half goes to their favorite charity. Getting a hole in one on national television *and* giving a huge donation to a charity, it doesn't get any better than that.

I had gotten used to playing in front of galleries and on television, and I even learned to embrace the experiences. Of course, in my early days this wasn't the case. Most of us get rattled when we have to play in front of strangers, let alone a television camera. But being an actress, playing golf for a television audience became just another role for me. Until now.

When I was offered the tournament I was pumped. As I said, my game was sharp then, and I actually thought I might win the amateur part of the event.

The key to a par 3, other than hitting the green on your first shot of course, is good putting. If you can putt, then par 3s are yours for the taking.

I worked hard on my putting during the weeks leading up to the tournament. Long putts, short putts, left to rights, right to lefts, uphill and downhill. If I looked at it, I was making it.

> Being over-confident can be hazardous to your health.

I think the biggest lesson I learned from this event was confidence. Rather, having too much of it. Being over-confident can be hazardous to your health. I put it that way because if the Surgeon General uses those words to scare people away from smoking, then that's good enough for me. Do not get me wrong—confidence is necessary in golf. However, learn how to keep it in perspective. Always.

This event was at the Aviara Golf Club at the Four Seasons Resort in Carlsbad, California. Visually it's one of the most beautiful places to be. It's adjacent to the Batiquitos Lagoon, a natural wildlife paradise filled with over a hundred types of birds. The path along the lagoon is so romantic you may want to renew your wedding vows right there on the spot.

I was going to be in a high-powered foursome: Freddie Couples, Johnny Miller, and Kelli Kuehne. Brian was going to caddy for me, and we were supposed to have a nice romantic weekend together, filled with spa treatments, long walks along the lagoon, and me winning the Par 3 Challenge. At least that is the way I envisioned it.

Little did I know that in a few hours, the ***love*** *was going to hit the fan.*

The day before the tournament, I played a practice round and hit almost every green on the course, the longest hole being around 160 yards. You had to hit the green or pay the price: the course was set up so that if you missed a green, you landed in the thickest rough known to golfers. It made the U.S. Open rough look as short as shag carpet.

After the practice round, Brian and I went back to the hotel for a candlelit dinner. We talked about what clubs I would hit on certain holes in the tournament the next day. Being a great husband means many things. It means never forgetting an anniversary or a birthday. It means knowing the perfect words to pick you up when you are down. However, most importantly, it means knowing the exact yardages you can hit with every club in your bag.

Afterwards, we took a walk along the lagoon, and it was as if we were on a second honeymoon. I was filled with love. Love for my husband and love for golf. I slept so peacefully that night. Little did I know that in a few hours, the *love* was going to hit the fan.

I got to the course bright and early to practice my putting. When I got there, I saw that something horrible had happened overnight. They had moved all the tee boxes back. *Way back.* The nerve! Suddenly the par 3s from my practice round were all fifty yards longer. This was no longer a par 3 challenge for me, it was a par 4 challenge!

I asked the tournament officials where all the nice par 3s from the practice round had gone. Get a load of what they told me next. All the holes had to be set up longer for the tournament because the *hole-in-one insurance* called for it. *What*? Hole-in-one insurance? What in heaven's name is that? I had never heard of it, and I am sure you haven't either. There is actually an insurance policy that guarantees that the million dollars is paid if someone gets an ace.

Brian said to them, "Look, she's playing with Freddie Couples, Johnny Miller, and Kelli Kuehne. I think the odds of one of them making a hole in one is better than Cheryl's. Why can't she just play from the tees that were used in the practice round?" No go. They would not budge.

With the new setup, I would be hitting my driver on practically every hole. I just did not think that was fair. I was an amateur in this event playing with professional golfers. There had to be some handicapping system used for the tee boxes where the pros hit from as opposed to the ones the amateurs use. It was like that at every other tournament, why not this one? With these yardages, I didn't have a chance. Well, that's not true, I did have a chance. A chance to be thoroughly humiliated on national television.

I thought for a few minutes about pulling out of the tournament. I could always go with that famous show business excuse, food poisoning. You've seen on those entertainment shows when a celebrity isn't able to attend an event they've agreed to, the excuse is usually food poisoning. It's a favorite in Hollywood.

I looked at Brian and was about to tell him that I did not want to play. He stopped me before I could get a word out. He knows me. He could see the fear in my eyes. Brian is great at talking me down. He knows just how to reassure me about anything. Women sometimes need reassurance about their relationship and occasionally about their golf game. This would be a good test for his reassurance skills. He started strong. "You've got the best short game I've ever seen! You can putt blindfolded! I've seen you make pars out of nowhere. Don't worry, you can do this." I took his advice and guess what? He lied. *Lied. Lied. Lied.* It was my darkest hour, or my darkest four hours, ever on a golf course. I didn't putt "lights out" like Brian says, I putted more like the lights *were* out. That was only half the problem. The distance just killed me. I missed almost every green and landed in the rough that surrounded each hole. It was virtually impossible for me to get out of it—unless my fourteenth club were a weed whacker. This wasn't the rough, it was velcro cabbage.

My group was very supportive, except their support had a reverse effect on me. The more encouragement they gave me, the worse I played. I could not hit a green to save my life. Even Kelli Kuehne couldn't get on some of these greens without hitting her 3-wood, and she's been a winner on the LPGA tour! She had a great positive attitude. Just like I once had. She made jokes and

Dazed and confused

kept the mood fun. On the occasions when she needed a wood, Kelli would just smile and say to her caddy, "Time to get out the furniture again." I walked off the course in tears and hid it well for the television cameras. I wanted you to see the look of panic on my face that day. Check out the picture of Johnny Miller offering his support: my ears were turned off at this point. Someone got a picture of Brian while he caddied for me on that fateful day. Look at his face. He did a lot of looking away that afternoon. I know how you feel, pal.

To this day if I'm at home and I get a call to play in a par 3 tournament I have only one swing thought: *let the answering machine get it.*

Brian feeling my pain

However, I walked away from the horror of that par 3 tournament with something very valuable: Johnny Miller's telephone number. He gave it to me after the last hole and said, "If you ever want some help with your golf or if there's anything I can do for you, here's my number. Don't be upset about your game today. That's what golf is. It's ups and downs. We have to remember that without any downs, we can't appreciate all the ups."

You're probably most familiar with Johnny from his job as the lead announcer for NBC golf. For my money, there's no better golf broadcaster out there. Johnny's open and fearless ability to speak his mind might rub some players the wrong way, but you have to love him for his honesty. It comes from his heart. He's a deeply spiritual man who follows where his faith leads him. A big part of that is being honest in his golf announcing. It's who he is.

As for the players who complain behind the scenes about his on-camera critique, they need to lighten up a little. Look, I understand their plight. In a way, I'm in the same boat with them when it comes to something like this. I'm an actress; if I get a bad review, I'm not going to be happy about it, but I'm also not going to call the newspaper that printed it to complain. I accept it and move on. The reviewers are merely doing their job—do I agree with them? Maybe yes, maybe no. But it's what they get paid to do.

> "Don't be upset about your game today. That's what golf is. It's ups and downs."

In August of 2004, my game was a little rusty.

Now as far as Johnny's PGA career goes, in case you're new to the game, the cliff notes on him are as follows: Hall of Fame member, twenty-five-year career, twenty-five wins, British Open and U.S. Open champion. In that victory, his most treasured, Johnny shot a final round sixty-three, the lowest in U.S. Open history. The following season he won eight times and was crowned PGA Tour Player of the Year. His desire and passion for competitive golf began to wane around the young age of twenty-nine, replaced by what he felt were stronger life values that required his full focus, mainly, his wife and six children.

Through the years, much has been written about why Johnny's passion faded so early. Most of the accounts were unfavorable. I suppose *it's OK* for people to write negative articles speculating about why he retired, but it's *not OK* for him to speak his mind about other golfers during his television broadcasts. *Go figure…*

In August of 2004, my game was a little rusty. More like, very rusty. Like a lot of us, I'd been on a busy work schedule and had lots of family things going on. So needless to say, I wasn't getting in much practice on my game. Each of the handful of times over the last three months when Brian and I did play ended with me saying somewhere around the twelfth hole, "You finish, I'm just going to ride in the cart for the rest of the round."

My swing was so out of whack that I needed more than just the normal tune-up Brian or my local teacher could offer. I needed to speak to a higher power. I was looking over some pictures to put in the book one evening and came across a shot of Johnny Miller in which he was giving me a lesson on the grip. That's when it hit me: Johnny Miller can fix my swing. I dug out his number and figured the next day I'd call him up. Just so you know, I realize how truly blessed golf has been to me. To be able to pick up the phone and talk to Johnny Miller about my golf swing is a gift you can't put a price tag on.

The next morning I spoke with his assistant. "I need Johnny's help."

"Sure thing, Cheryl. Is everything OK?"

"Well, I'm OK, but my swing's not OK. It's more like O with flashes of K. But never O and K at the same time. I need Johnny."

She just laughed; obviously he's bombarded with requests all day long. But that's for a good reason. Johnny is one of the good eggs who will give you his number because he wants you to call him, especially if he can help out. He's a born teacher. In his own words about his sometimes instructive broadcasting style, he says, "I love teaching so much, I'm actually giving a lesson on TV. I will never just say, 'He hit that shot terribly, he's choking.' I might insinuate it, but I'll also tell how he corrects it. So I complete the circle. My theory is, I hope he's watching or his dad's watching or his teacher's watching. It's my way of educating."

My educating would come a few hours later when Johnny returned my panicked swing call. That morning I was so excited to get my telephone lesson that Brian and I went over to the local

Cheryl and Johnny Miller

Radio Shack to buy the little doohickey that you connect to the receiver to tape-record phone calls. I needed to have this lesson for posterity. After all, it's not every day that you get a lesson from Johnny Miller. I'll skip the "Hi, how have you been?" stuff and get right to the meat of the conversation. Or the tofu for you veggie golfers . . .

Here's how it went.

"Hi Cheryl, I hear your swing needs a little fixing. What's the problem? Or should I ask, what are the problems?"

"Problems, you're right. I'll start where all my problems begin, with my grip. I can't seem to get a good feel in my grip lately."

"As far as grips go, they're like going to Baskin-Robbins. It's hard to say one flavor is better than another. All three grip styles are good—interlock, overlap, and ten-finger. It's whatever feels comfortable to you. But I do feel that once you decide on a grip, you should follow these steps. Are you writing this down?"

"Actually, I'd like to tape your call. Do you mind?"

"Sure, go ahead. OK, I would say the main thing about a woman is that when you grip the club pay close attention to the Vs on the right hand. The V on a man's tour grip generally points to our right ear. Now, for a woman, if you look at the LPGA Tour players, it's a little stronger, more between the right ear and the shoulder. I think all women should have their grip a little stronger for several reasons. Tell me, have you also noticed a loss of distance?"

"Yes!"

"Thought so; I remember you hitting the ball a good distance. We'll fix it. By strengthening your grip, you line up your left elbow, tricep, and deltoid muscles better. With a stronger grip and by incorporating those muscles, you'll have greater pulling strength through impact with the ball. A stronger grip lets you pull more and hit the ball harder. It allows the hands to lead the club through, not vice versa. The weaker the left-hand

I've met many basketball greats at the different tournaments I'm in. Here, Brian and I are with the legendary Julius Erving. I've put this picture in to actually give you a golf tip. Look at how big Dr. J's and Brian's hands are. In order for them to hold a golf club correctly, their grips are bigger than standard. As a general rule, chronic slicers should never use oversized grips, and chronic hookers should never use undersized grips. Here's how you can check: for right-handed golfers, hold your club in your left hand. A properly fitted grip size should cause the fingernails of the left hand to dig slightly into the palm when holding the grip. If your hands are small like mine, use an undersized grip; if they're large, use a slightly oversized grip. Golf grips cost around three bucks each installed. Get yours checked—it's worth it. In a related note, I'll leave you with this question: since ball players hands are so huge, do you think they can use a regular knife and fork, or do they need bigger utensils?

Each of these poor swings is the result of the same flaw, an overactive right hand. During my follow-through in all three of these pictures, my right hand is taking control of my swing. It's a natural tendency for anyone who's right-handed. On the downswing/follow-through, you want to pull the club through with your left hand and not allow your right hand to "chop" at the ball.

grip is, the less the pulling muscles will work and the more the right hand will overpower the left on the downswing. You'll have less pulling strength, giving you a loss in power and distance. That's why on the LPGA Tour, the grips are generally stronger. Now that you're going to incorporate a stronger grip and stronger pulling action through the ball, this is going to help you hit crisper shots. One of the things I stress with female golfers is at the bottom of their swing, they should make a nice 'crisp' hit and try to brush the grass. The most common problem I see with female amateurs is that they get a little loose with their grip at the bottom of their swing, and they're not crisp through the ball. They get dainty and wave at the ball rather than striking through it."

"So a stronger grip can help with gaining distance?"

"Yes. Another way to bring your distance back is to take note of what the longest hitters do, like Nicklaus. In Jack's backswing, all of his power was loaded and geared up on his right side, so

Before the fall

when he came at the ball, he'd be hitting it with all he's got. At the top of his swing when he changed direction, you could see that the ball was going to get walloped."

"Are there any swing thoughts you can suggest for this?"

"I would try to remember that six inches before you hit the ball, make sure you mean business. Gear up all your muscles in your body to get ready for the strike, firm up your grip for the moment of contact. Don't stiffen up—firm up your muscles. This way your ball will travel on a nice line with spin, rather than having a little rainbow shot. It's very much the same mentality as karate. Stay relaxed till you make the strike."

Those are some excellent thoughts from the mind of one the greatest golfers of all time. We talked some more, and I was telling him about my book and he was talking about his book *I Call the Shots*, which had just come out. Then he asked me if he could mention something in particular for all the token chicks out there. Johnny is a big believer in husbands and wives playing golf together—that it's great for a relationship. Here's what he said.

"Most couples raise their kids, then get to fifty or so and the kids are gone, and you're both looking at each other one day thinking, do I know you? Do we have anything in common? Golf is such a great way to spend time together, walking, enjoying the outdoors, eating together afterwards—it's all-inclusive. Plus with the handicap system and tee boxes set up for the different players, you can enjoy friendly competition with your partner. I can honestly say that some of the strongest marriages I've ever seen are ones where the husband and wife golf together. It's truly a great way for couples to enjoy the second stage of their lives with one another, or should I say, enjoy the back nine of their lives together."

That's pretty poetic, don't you think? After I thanked him for his time and his tips, he said, "Cheryl, you don't have to thank me. One more thing, if you and Brian ever want to come up for some golf at Pebble Beach, just let me know and I'll take care of it for you. It's so romantic there, it's like a second honeymoon—you'd both love it."

I'm sure glad I came across that number. Brian and I are definitely going to take him up on that double-date golf offer and possibly that second honeymoon.

TOKEN TIPS

Even though that par 3 tournament was the low point in my golf life, I wanted to share with you one of the highest points of my golf life. It also involves a par 3—only this par 3 gave me a hole in one. Brian and I were golfing with our friend, tennis great Jimmy Connors. We were at our home course near Santa Barbara, and it was one of those days where there wasn't a gust of wind or a cloud in the sky. Simply perfect. We got to the ninth hole, a 145-yard par 3. I pulled a 5-iron from my bag and looked at the hole. It was the first time I had actually *visualized* my shot. I closed my eyes and pictured how I would swing and how the ball would fly. Just hit the green, I told myself. That's your goal. I said a quick prayer, opened my eyes, and hit my shot. I watched the ball soar to the green and bent down to pick up my tee. My ball landed and Jimmy yelled, "Cheryl! Look!" I lifted my head and saw the ball

TOKEN SIDE TIP Remember, there's a huge amount of luck in getting a hole in one. So if you manage to get one, on your way home from the golf course, buy a lottery ticket. Hey, no one ever expects to get a hole in one, it just happens. Who knows, that same blessing might carry over and give you the winning lottery jackpot ticket.

bounce once, twice, and then disappear as if the green had swallowed it. "A hole in one! A hole in one!" Brian shouted. He and Jimmy were more excited than I was—I was too stunned to even believe that it happened—but when I got to the green and saw that ball in the bottom of the cup, I was speechless.

Closing my eyes before I hit and visualizing my shot helped me to stay relaxed through my swing and gave me a goal, hitting the green. Getting it in the hole was of course a total bonus. It's important to watch every shot land after you've hit it. If not for Jimmy yelling for me to look, I would have missed seeing my hole in one.

"A hole in one!
A hole in one!"
Brian shouted.

THE F WORD

There are conflicting opinions about what the first lesson of golf should be. Is it about the fundamentals? How to grip, stand, and swing the club? Maybe it should be about etiquette. I learned about golf etiquette the first time Brian and I played with two strangers. It was probably our third or fourth time out, and we'd been paired with two older men. The hundred name tags from courses all over the world they each had hanging from their hundred-year-old golf bags informed all strangers that they played a lot.

At the first tee the practice swings Brian and I were taking showed something loud and clear. Beginners. One of the men asked, "How long have you two been playing?"

"We just took it up," I said happily.

"Rookies."

Rookies? Brian jumped in to defend us.

“I’m Scottish.”

“Uh-huh, what about her?”

“She’s an actress but can play Scottish. Quite well I might add.”

They laughed at that, and then one of them recognized me. He asked the classic question when someone recognizes a celebrity but can’t remember their name. “Are you who I think you are?”

You have to help them out here. You extend your hand and say, “Yes, I am. I’m Cheryl, nice to meet you.” I’ve now given them a fifty-fifty chance. “Oh, yeah, you’re Cheryl Tiegs, you’re great.” Sometimes it’s easier to just go with it, “Thank you very much.”

At the first tee, one of the guys said to pay attention to them during the round. That we might learn something from these veterans of the links. In other words, *Watch it rookies or hit the (cart path) pavement.*

On the first green came my first lesson in golf etiquette. One of the men was lining up his putt when I walked directly in his line. He made sure to tell me. Or at least he made sure to clear his throat at me.

“Ahem?”

“Yes?”

“Line.”

“Ahh, to be or not to be?”

“Not that line. You walked in my line.”

“I’m sorry. Is that bad?”

"Yes."

"How bad?"

"Not that bad. Just don't do it again."

"Does it cost me any penalty strokes?"

"Not yet."

We learned a lot of golf etiquette that day with those two men. Everything we needed to know. And all before the fifth hole.

Wrap your arms over your head, crunch your back, and recite any prayer that comes to mind immediately.

Another rule in golf is to listen for the *F* word. When you hear it, make sure you do the *D* word. The F word is "fore" and the D word is "duck." There's actually a plan you should follow when you hear the F word yelled from anywhere on the course. Wrap your arms over your head, crunch your back, and immediately recite any prayer that comes to mind.

Normally when you hear "fore," it's from the group playing behind you or maybe someone from another fairway. Very rarely does it happen the way I've seen it happen, let alone twice. I'm talking about the rare times when there isn't even a chance to yell "fore."

Brian and I had just arrived in Hawaii at the Mauna Lani Resort and were paired with two local men. Both were good golfers who had each driven the ball consistently straight for the first nine holes. We got to the tenth hole, and the ladies' tee box was set up way to the left of the men's. It was a good thirty yards ahead of theirs, but definitely out in their sightline.

On every hole prior to this one, I had waited for the men to tee off and then walked ahead to the ladies' tees to hit my shot. However, on this hole since the ladies' tees were off to the left and thirty yards ahead, I decided to walk over and wait in my own tee box for them to hit. The first man up also happened to be the best golfer in our group. I saw him take his backswing, and at the same moment, the golf voice in my head started yelling at me to watch out! Under normal conditions when the golf voice in our head starts talking, we do our best to tune it out. Usually it's saying something like, "Don't slice," or "Don't miss this putt." But today the golf voice in my head was my friend. No negativity. The golf voice had one mission, to protect where it lives. Inside my head.

The ball nailed me in the back of my thigh, the stinging pain took a few seconds to travel up to my brain, then when it reached there, it sent back down the message to my legs. ***Collapse.***

Right before he made contact with the ball, the voice in my head *screamed* at me to turn around, cover my head with my arms, and crouch. That left him a nice target to aim at.

He hit his tee shot, and the ball came at me with the precise aim that a sniper would have. It nailed me and knocked me to the ground. I now know what it feels like when a boxer in the ring gets hit with a knockout punch, then takes a few seconds to hit the canvas. That's what happened to me. The ball nailed me in the back of my thigh, the stinging pain took a few seconds to travel up to my brain, then when it reached there, it sent back down the message to my legs. *Collapse.*

The two men argued on the tee about whether he should take a mulligan or play the ball where it lay. Thanks a lot!

Luckily, the ball found the one spot on my body that would spare me from being severely injured. I had always wondered why God gave me a little extra padding there—now I know why. Brian came running over to see if I was OK, while the two men argued on the tee about whether he should take a mulligan or play the ball where it lay. Thanks a lot! I finished my round limping and throbbing the whole way.

Brian and I had made a deal on this trip. One day golf, one day swimming pool, one day golf, one day shopping, and so on. Since yesterday was golf, today's schedule would either be the pool or shopping. We decided on the pool.

I changed into my bathing suit, and Brian looked at my backside and his shoulders fell. Not the look you want from your husband when you've just put on a brand-new seventy-dollar bathing suit that *you* thought looked great. "Honey, we can't go to the swimming pool."

"Why? This is a brand-new bathing suit! I think it looks great."

"Sure the suit is great, but turn around and take a look."

Those are fighting words. Was he telling me that there was something wrong with my butt? Before I got my lawyer on the phone ready to sue my husband for slander, I looked in the mirror and saw the most ghastly glowing purple welt the size of a grapefruit on my thigh. "We can't go to the pool with a bruise like that. People are going to think I'm beating you. I guess we have to go shopping."

Brian looked bummed out. He likes the pool, can tolerate shopping, but loves golf. I said the only thing I could to make his shoulders bounce right back up. "Forget the shopping, forget the pool, I have just the idea for this vacation. Thirty-six holes a day!"

The lesson I learned is that when the golf voice in your head is talking to you, don't block it out, listen to what it has to say. It might be important. Unless, of course, it's telling you not to miss a two-footer. If that's the case, tell it to *shut up!*

But if not for the voice in my head, I would have been nailed by that tee shot—whether he yelled "fore" or not. The next person I saw get hit with a ball also didn't have the luxury of hearing "fore." The voice in her head didn't tell her to duck. A bigger voice from above *made* her stand where she was and get hit by the ball. And for good reason: to save her life.

The lesson I learned is that when the golf voice in your head is talking to you, don't block it out.

Brian and I were playing at the Lakes Golf and Country Club in Palm Desert. They have three nine-hole courses, and twenty-two of the twenty-seven holes have water hazards. So if you visit there, make sure to bring lots and lots of balls. (Token chick side note: Palm Desert in California is a great romantic golf getaway for couples.) The signature hole on the north course is a 155-yard par 3 over water, but I think they may want to change the reason why it's their signature hole.

Brian and I were enjoying the other couple, and everything was completely normal until that signature hole. The pin was way in the back corner, and the whipping wind suggested that a nice shot that faded slightly right would land near the cup. The woman and I teed off and were just happy to land near the green.

Brian hit and he landed safely on the center of the green. The other man was next to tee off. He threw some blades of grass into the air, and after judging that the wind was coming at us (I could have told him that), he then studied his bag as to which club he'd hit. After the long decision was made, he pulled his club. A 6-iron. I only know what club it was because when he took it out of his bag, he told everyone, "Lucky 6-iron." He didn't even know how lucky it would become.

He was one of those golfers who talk out loud when they make decisions on the golf course. "Lucky 6-iron. I'll hit a high fade and work it over to the hole. Here we go."

He gripped his club and took a wacky stance over the ball. One leg was forward, the other leg was back, his upper body was facing way left, his head was looking to the right—it all looked fundamentally wrong. But what do I know, I can't hit a high fade; maybe this was how you do it. He said once more, to remind everyone that we were about to see greatness unfold, "High fade and I'll work it over to the hole." He looked at the hole and adjusted his wacky stance a tad more. He gave the hole one final look and then hit away.

His ball headed straight for his wife. He hit a violent shank. ("Shank" is the single worst word in golf. It basically means you hit a horrible shot that went sideways.) His shot hit her straight in the kisser. It was gruesome. She hit the ground, and the ball knocked almost every tooth out of her mouth. Blood was gushing everywhere, and we rushed her back to the clubhouse where an ambulance took her and her husband to the hospital. Golf was done for the day.

"You know something, hitting her with that ball was the best day of my life."

A few days later, Brian and I saw that same man at the putting green, laughing and having a good time. *What the*—? He hit his wife in the mouth and knocked her teeth out seventy-three hours ago, and now he's back at the course having a grand time? He saw us and walked over with a huge smile and a handshake.

"Hi, thanks for everything the other day."

"How's your wife? Is she going to be OK?"

"You know something, hitting her with that ball was the best day of my life."

What? I was almost ready to hit him with my club after that remark, but I gave him a chance to explain first.

"Best day in her life, too."

Now I'm really confused, but he explained. "We got to the hospital, and they X-rayed her head to see what the damage was. That X-ray showed she had a brain tumor. The doc said that if it hadn't been discovered when it was, she would have been dead in three months."

He saved his wife's life by hitting a shank and not yelling "fore." Like Bob Hope used to say, "Shank you very much."

Golf is such a mental game, it's scary.

Thankfully I've never hit anyone (yet) with a golf ball and if I ever do, I hope something life-saving comes out of it. Now just because I never hit a person, that doesn't mean I haven't hit something else. I was playing in an LPGA event at the Ibis Golf and Country Club in West Palm Beach, Florida. They have three fantastic Jack Nicklaus–designed courses there that are next to the Grassy Waters Nature Preserve. While you're golfing, it's not unusual to see exotic wildlife strolling the course.

Florida is headquarters to both the PGA and LPGA, and whenever a tournament rolls into town, you can expect a big turnout. I was standing at the first tee taking my practice swings as my name was announced to the gallery. I was smiling to the fans, when out of the corner of my eye I saw a bird that looked straight out of *Jurassic Park*. They're called sandhill cranes. They stand about four feet tall, have long skinny legs and a wingspan of over seven feet. Fossils of them date back over six million years, making them the oldest still-living species of birds. They live mostly in the Midwest, and as soon as the summer ends, they migrate to Florida for the winter months. As they should—being a species that old qualifies you for retirement, and there's no better place for that than Florida. Oh, one last thing, they're endangered. Great, just my luck.

I teed up my ball and kept staring at the sandhill crane. I was determined to not let it be a distraction, but someone forgot to tell my golf swing that. Golf is such a mental game, it's scary. It's happened to every golfer on the course: whether there's water, bunkers, or a sandhill crane, we focus so much on avoiding the obstacle that it acts like a magnet pulling your shot directly at it. I aimed as far away from the bird as I could. There was going to be no way that I would hit it. But, instead of my tee shot sailing onto the fairway, I hit a low-burning Scud missile that was heading straight for the bird.

I dropped my club and put my hands over my mouth, muffling my gasp.

To me, the whole thing was happening in slow motion. I could see the gallery's faces fill with horror as the ball was rocketing toward this defenseless creature. Some people had physical reactions as if my ball were heading toward them. They were actually ducking out of the way for the crane, maybe hoping the bird would see them and catch on in a split second.

My ball hit the bird, and the thud sound it made was horrific. I'll have to check with the Guinness Book of World Records, but I think it was the largest gasp ever made by a crowd. I dropped my club and put my hands over my mouth, muffling my gasp. The few seconds that passed seemed like minutes. Everyone was frozen. Me, the gallery, and the bird.

The gallery held its collective breath waiting for the poor creature to crumple, but no. Instead, it turned and glared at me like I was pond scum. Right before he strutted off, he lifted his wing and held it in the air. He flipped me off! That bird had just given me the bird!

TOKEN TIPS

The reason I hit that bird was because I was focusing so much on *not* hitting it. Getting freaked out about a hazard, water, bunkers, or sandhill cranes is more common than getting a cold in the winter. There's a mental approach you can take when faced with these shots. I actually got this tip when I was playing golf one day with a psychiatrist. He said, "Most people simply need to change their mind-set about hazards." This is what he recommended: When you're faced with hitting your shot over any hazard, don't think to yourself, *I don't want to hit it in the water.* Instead, think to yourself, *I want to hit it over the water.* Sounds almost too simple, but it works!

TOKEN SIDE TIP If the doc's tip doesn't work, just remember, he didn't charge you for the visit.

FIJI

"I love you" are the three most beautiful words on earth. The next three words that fall into that category are, *The Wakaya Club.* And the three words that follow that are, *Pack your bags!* But you mustn't pack too much because the small plane that takes you to this hideaway only allows ninety-five pounds of luggage per person.

The Wakaya Club is a private retreat in the middle of the Fiji islands. I classify it in the "retreat" bracket, since it has nine cottages and the island only accommodates a maximum of twenty guests at a time. It's neither a hotel nor a resort, it's a paradise of romance and bliss. A *retreat*.

How much so? When the richest man in the world, Bill Gates, took his bride on their honeymoon, they went to Wakaya. I've read that the house he lives in costs a hundred million dollars, and he chose this spot for his honeymoon. I don't know if you can get a better endorsement than that. "Hi, I'm the richest man in the world and I don't get away from the office that often, but when I do, I go to Wakaya."

Even the air in the South Pacific gives you a sort of balance. Its theme is *peace and piece*. As in *peace and quiet, piece of mind, inner peace*. That's what it was for Tom Cruise and Nicole Kidman. When they were married it was their getaway: *peace and quiet*. When they got divorced, they had two weeks that had been booked earlier that year so they decided to split them, one week for each: *piece of mind*. But Wakaya's atmosphere lends itself to those who want to put ill feelings behind them. Three years after the split, they gave their children a special Christmas gift. They booked every room at Wakaya and all shared a family Christmas vacation together: *inner peace*.

The man who built this kingdom of paradise is named David Gilmour. He's on a different level from your normal hotel mogul. He figures out how to make your trip to his palace a once-in-a-lifetime personal experience like no other. It's the real-life version of *Fantasy Island*. Celine Dion is a frequent guest and says, "When you leave, you cry."

The personal fantasy for me came true when Brian and I got to the golf course they have on the property and saw a plaque hanging with the course name on it. It was engraved *The Cheryl Ladd International Golf Course*. They knew I loved golf and was one of the first to play their course, so they bestowed the ultimate tribute on me: my very own golf course.

The golf course is nine holes, about fourteen hundred yards long, and it's built on a nineteenth-century coconut grove. This also makes for the toughest hazard on the course. The coconut trees that line the fairways keep you edgy and cautious on each backswing. Without warning, a coconut could fall and zonk you in the head. This was serious business to me since my name's on the course. What if Bill Gates is golfing and gets knocked out by a falling coconut and gets amnesia? I'm sure there'd be some angry stockholders knocking at my door. I asked the greenskeeper/starter/instructor if anyone had ever been beaned in the beanie by a coconut. His answer would sound insane anywhere but there. In some parts of the world, you have to go with what the locals tell you, and he told us, "The eyes of a coconut make sure that they never hit anyone and split open their head." Whatever that means . . .

Without warning, a coconut could fall and zonk you in the head.

The next day we played nine holes and turned right around and played them again. We were walking back to our cottage past the tennis courts when we saw the only other guests on the island that week. They were an older couple who were well into their eighties, although their energy didn't resemble their age. They were good tennis players. The man was a type of tennis player I had never seen before. He had a cigarette dangling from his mouth while he was volleying with his wife.

I've seen all types of smokers in my time, but he seemed to puff with a passion. He had obviously been smoking his whole life, and he needed it on the tennis court in his eighties as much as he did on the handball court as a teen.

That night we talked with them before dinner.

"We saw you walking in from the golf course. How was your round today?"

"Fantastic. How was your tennis?"

"Excellent."

I asked them, "Do you two play golf? Would you care to join us for a round in the morning?" I really wanted them to play with us. They were the only other guests there, and I wanted them to see the plaque at the course with my name on it. Wouldn't you?

"We don't golf anymore; it's too slow for us."

You have to love people in their eighties describing something as being too slow.

"Would you like to join us for tennis instead?"

Brian and I used to play tennis but that was before golf. When we fell in love with golf, we hung up our tennis racquets. Golf is like all other loved ones. They don't like it when you do something behind their back. Especially playing tennis.

Since there was no one else on the island, we thought it was the right thing to do, so we agreed to meet them for doubles.

We met them the next day in the lobby, and the old man lit up a smoke the moment he set foot outdoors. By the time we had taken the ninety-second walk to the tennis courts, he was finishing up his third cigarette. The couple asked us if we wanted to warm up, hit a few balls, and maybe have a smoke. Brian and I hit balls for about, ohh, three minutes while the old man drank water and smoked two more cigarettes. One in each hand. That was *his* warm-up.

The first game against these geezers ended quickly. For Brian and me, that is. So did the second, third, and fourth. They were running us ragged in every direction on the court, to the point where we couldn't breathe. We were huffing and the chain-smoking old guy was puffing. Brian and I needed a team meeting. We needed some strategy, but more importantly, we needed oxygen. We were down four games to zip in all of five minutes time.

We stood at the back of the tennis court like two boxers desperately stealing a moment to regain their composure right before they get knocked out. Brian was breathing so fast that he could barely get out his words, "Honey, are you trying?"

"Trying! I'm trying my ass off! Are you trying?"

"What the hell is going on, they're twice our age!"

For our next set the old man decided to kick his play up a notch. He charged the net with his cigarette dangling and drilled ball after ball past us. Then, Brian finally lost his composure and started to return every shot he could with an overhead smash directly at the smoker's elderly wife. She wouldn't flinch. She wouldn't go down—and she was over eighty. *Excuse me, what's wrong with this picture?* They kicked our golf butts severely that morning.

When the horror ended and the (secondhand) smoke had finally cleared, we'd learned a very inspirational lesson from our elders. When you're too old for golf, there's always tennis!

I also discovered an interesting link among the owner, the Cheryl Ladd International Golf Course, the retreat, the ocean, the old couple, and how I account for their energy.

Years ago while standing at the second hole of the golf course bearing my name at the paradise he owned, David saw some of his guests drinking bottled water. Water that had been imported from halfway across the world. Just to inform you, Fiji has the most sheltered ecosystem on earth. In English, this means "it's perfect." David was already bottling the Fiji water and serving it exclusively to his Wakaya guests. He wanted to make it available to the rest of the world and he did. He's the guy who created the bottled water called Fiji. Well, God created the water, but it was David's idea to put it in that cool square bottle. How does the old couple that whooped Brian and me figure into this equation? The old couple kept drinking water during our tennis match, and I am now convinced that the pure-ecosystem Fiji water is actually the Fountain of Youth!

TOKEN TIPS

When you're golfing in a hot climate, whether it be the desert, Florida in the summer, or even Fiji, you need to remain hydrated. That's the fancy expression for, "Drink lots of water!" Bodies need gallons of water to stay hydrated in summer heat. Heat sickness is fast acting and dangerous. Heat cramps, heat exhaustion, and heatstroke can bring about an irreversible coma and even death. I know it sounds dramatic, but it can be.

It's easier to take steps to prevent heatstroke than it is to treat it. Most doctors recommend drinking eight or more glasses of water a day during normal weather conditions and twice that during high-heat periods. When the temperatures go past ninety degrees and the humidity levels climb, you can lose a couple of pounds in an hour if you are working hard outside. I know this may sound tempting to some of you, but it's not a good way to lose weight. On the golf course during hot days, try to drink four ounces of water every two holes. Professional athletes drink loads of water and sports drinks when they play and practice; we weekend warriors need to do the same.

TOKEN SIDE TIP Now that you're going to be drinking more water, take note of the most important holes on the course: the ones that have a restroom.

GOLF IS A FOUR-LETTER WORD

Golf is a four-letter word in more ways than one. We have all sunk into the dark realm of using bad language when we're playing lousy. Sometimes using it, though, is the only way to get through a round. However, I am going to focus here on a different four-letter word that is more on the feminine side. You guys have *your* four-letter words; this is about *our* four-letter word, *love*. Playing golf is doing something you love, therefore you should be doing it *with* the person you love or may love in the near future.

If you have not golfed with your significant other, what are you waiting for? Are you a self-imposed golf widow living in exile while the rest of us feast on all its riches? I know I am sounding a bit dramatic, but girls, listen up. Golfing with my husband has been such a positive benefit to our relationship that I cannot even remember what we did *before* we started golfing.

A round of golf is a perfect **second** date, not a first date.

After you finish this chapter, either get out there with your guy and play or get on the phone and start booking your tee times. If you're both beginning golfers and don't know how to get it going, go to your local driving range and ask about taking lessons together.

In addition, while you are there, get some rental clubs and hit a bucket of balls. The newfound fun you can have is great for your relationship. Here is an example: Brian and I like to gamble sometimes on the course. However, our bets are not about money. They are about quiet dinners, deep massages, and other things. You get the point . . .

Golf can also be very informative when you are getting into a new relationship. If you are looking for a new love, playing a round of golf with someone you're considering is like used-car shopping. It's important to bring a used car to a mechanic before you buy it. You want to find out if he, I mean, the *car*, needs any major repairs. That's what playing golf with potential mates is like. After one round, you will know if this guy is worth keeping or if you need to keep on used-car shopping.

A round of golf is a perfect *second* date, not a first date. On a first date if it is going badly, you may need to bail out. That's tough to pull off if you're on the fifth hole and you hate him already. Besides, your nerves are racing enough on the typical first date; I do not think you need to throw a round of golf into the fire. So make it a second or third date. After that round, take the information you have learned and use the questions below as a barometer to see what makes him tick.

The first and most obvious is: *Does he have a temper? Is he yelling and cursing on the course?* If he is, it is likely he will be yelling and cursing off the course too.

There is no tolerating a cheater.

If you have a borderline gimme putt, will he always give it to you? Is he supportive, does he give you encouragement? If the answer's *yes*, then consider bringing him home to meet your family. He shows good, strong values. You should also expect him to open your car door. Could be a keeper.

Is he overly helpful? This is a tough one. It can go either way. Usually if they're overly helpful they tend to be a little controlling. But there's always the possibility that they're just *being* helpful. The only advice I can offer on this one is the same as if you were buying a golf glove. *If it feels right, then get it.*

And last but certainly not least: *does he cheat?* That one stinks. Generally if they cheat on the golf course, they're liars somewhere in their personal life. Golf is based in personal integrity. There is no tolerating a cheater. Remember what your parents said, "They never profit."

So get some golf into your relationship, girl! It doesn't matter if you're with someone or looking for someone. It just works. It's

It's powerful—as powerful as love itself.

a good thing. It's powerful—as powerful as love itself. Sometimes it can even *over*power the power of love. Quick example: Let's say my best friend, Ann, has just met the man of her dreams, the guy she's been waiting for her whole life. Now let's also say that when Ann was playing golf last week she got a hole in one. If I'm introducing Ann to a friend, am I going to say, "This is Ann, she just met the man of her dreams." Or, "This is Ann, she got a hole in one last week!" See, it overpowers the power of love. Case closed.

TOKEN TIPS

If your significant other is a golfer and you want to get him a gift, here's a good suggestion. Golf balls are usually the first choice, but if you want to be a little different, get them personalized. Every ball manufacturer will imprint any message you want on golf balls, and it doesn't cost a lot. You can order personalized golf balls from any golf catalog company or online or even in your local store.

TOKEN SIDE TIP Personalized golf balls are a great way to get across your message. Both ends of the spectrum work, from "Stop leaving the toilet seat up" to "Are you ever going to propose?"

THE KING AND I

My golf life is complete. If I packed away my clubs tomorrow (not happening, by the way . . .), I could say that all my golf dreams have been fulfilled. Fulfilled, that is, because of one governing factor. Getting to play golf with Arnold Palmer. Instead of me spending sixty pages rambling on about him, I've decided to go with a few single words that define him.

Gentleman. Sexy. Gifted. Sincere. Captivating. Humble. Exciting. Fierce. Sexy. Hero.

You'll notice that I put in the word *sexy* twice. That's because he's twice as sexy as mere mortal men. He's utterly charming. Not Prince Charming, *King* Charming.

When I was a little girl, playing golf certainly wasn't *cool*. But then came Arnie. He wasn't like other golfers. He was one of us. His fans followed him loyally on their television screens and on the course. His army. He was a swashbuckler in a pale blue cardigan. He's the grandson of the golf gods, and they follow him every step he takes. I had one of my greatest moments ever on a golf course when I played with Arnie.

It was during the pro-am at Bighorn Golf Club in Palm Desert, California. You may have seen this course on television—it's where Tiger Woods brought golf to prime-time television for his "Battle at Bighorn" matches. Tiger had the course set up with tremendous flood lights so the closing holes could be played at night. (When can they get some street lights over at my home course?)

Arnie and I were playing with three other men. These three were shaking all day after their initial hellos with Arnie. Can you blame them? You don't want to hit a bad shot when you're playing with the King. It's almost disrespectful. As for my game that day, the least amount of pressure was on me. I played very well that afternoon. I've learned from the pro-ams that when you're the woman, especially when you're the *Token Chick*, no one really expects you to play that well. So if I have an OK round, everyone's impressed. If I have a good round, they think I should turn pro.

We got to a par 3 that had an elevated tee to a tiny green surrounded by mountains and rocks. You had to hit the green or your shot would bounce off the terrain like it was in a pinball

machine. Arnie went first, and he hit it to about fifteen feet from the cup. Would you expect anything less? The other three men in our group went next. With precise synchronized timing, one of them hooked his ball to the left, the other sprayed his shot to the right, and the last one topped his ball and landed short in the rocks.

Now it was my turn. For the first time that day, I started to shake a little in my (golf) boots.

I remember thinking that if these three guys couldn't get on the dance floor then what chance did I have? I looked down below at the green and it actually *shrank* while I looked at it. Then I got a glimpse of the gallery. They actually *grew* while I looked at them. It seemed like thousands of people were sitting and surrounding this green. Thank goodness for them. No, not because my tee shot hit one of them and my ball landed on the green as a result. It's because they're golf fans. They saw me standing in the tee box and could sense my anxiety. Like true fans of the game, they started shouting. "C'mon, Cheryl, you can do it!!!" I fed off that energy. I gave myself a swing thought based on motivation

and nothing else. I had trusted my swing all day, no need to stop now. What I needed was a mental boost. I thought, *Cheryl, you're a golfer and an actor. Act like a golfer.* They must have heard me talking to myself, because the crowd suddenly got louder: "C'mon, Cheryl, you can do it! Knock it stiff!"

I teed up my ball, lined up the shot, and swung away. The ball sailed in the air and gently floated down to about eight feet from the cup inside of Arnie's ball. The crowd went crazy! They were cheering like college football fans, but someone was even more excited. It was Arnie. He was way past thrilled. The look on his face was so . . . pure. I think he appreciates good shots from his amateur partners for another reason. He knows that he's Arnold Palmer and that every golfer from amateur to professional who shakes his hand idolizes him. He understands that you're under pressure playing alongside him. Therefore, he appreciates your effort. When Arnie congratulated me on my shot, I was speechless. I still couldn't believe that I had actually hit such a good shot under those circumstances right in front of His Highness. Token chick moment if ever there was one.

We all headed down to the green, and the crowd was still cheering. The marshals held the people off to either side as Arnie made his way toward the green. Since I was last to tee off, I was last to arrive at the green. Arnie was standing there waiting for me. He put his arms in the air to silence the cheers. Like the loyal soldiers they are that make up Arnie's army, they do whatever their general asks. Everyone hushed and Arnie introduced me to the crowd. "Please welcome the woman who hit that spectacular shot, Cheryl Ladd." He then gestured for their applause. The ovation was thunderous. It echoed off the mountainside, and it sounded like we were having an earthquake. Every actor will agree that there's nothing like the rush of applause from an audience. Your body tingles. But golf applause is different. It's better. It's from those who can relate.

I still couldn't believe that I had actually hit such a good shot under those circumstances right in front of His Highness.

Arnie then took my hand and escorted me on to the green. The crowd quieted and fell silent as he lined up and hit his putt. He left it a little right, but gave me the line. I drained my putt for the birdie, and the cheers picked up right where they left off.

I swear, after that experience, you couldn't be near me for two weeks without having to hear that story. He made me feel like a queen that day. Which comes so naturally to him—after all, he is the King.

Why Arnold is sexy . . . He just IS. It doesn't matter what type of look you're attracted to. Arnie is hot and token chicks can't resist him. I have some photographic proof.

Exhibit A

I don't think that this woman was aware that *I* was Arnie's girlfriend on the golf course that afternoon. With my husband's blessings, I may add. As you can see, she's moving right in on my man. *How dare she!* Giving him one of those, "Oooh, Arnie, you're so wonderful, can I have a hug," lines. FEH! I refused to stand for this. My body English speaks loud and clear. Look at what I mean. This golf groupie moves in on Arnie, I see it and turn my head fast enough to make my ponytail swoop. Now, look at my hands. My left hand is already making a fist ready to take out the competition and my right hand is crushing my golf ball. I needed to win my man back!

Exhibit B

Here we can see that I have to resort to strong tactics to win Arnie back. I put my token chick thinking cap on and used one of the oldest tricks in the playbook. After Arnie hugged the mystery woman, I jumped in with the classic line, "Hey, where's *my* hug?" Works every time . . .

Exhibit C

Success! This nice woman has graciously accepted the fact that *I* am Arnie's official girl for the day. Even Brian's expression tells a story, "Well, you put up a good fight, kid, but my wife knows how to chip, pitch, and woo." Brian's wonderful. He knows how much I love him and that he's my husband no matter what. *But*, if we're playing golf and Arnold Palmer is part of our group, *well*, I'm Arnie's girl that day. Arnie gave me a big hug, a croucher. When a man crouches to hug you, that's warm. Take a look at Brian, he's proud that his wife is Arnie's girl for the day. The *other* woman is smiling also and taking it on the chin like a true lady. Golf really does bring out the best in us girls. *Meow . . .*

TWO Js

In 2003, I made my return to network television on the NBC show *Las Vegas*. When I got the offer to do it, certainly I was excited, but that excitement went sky-high when I heard who my costar would be. James Caan. It's not too often that you get to act alongside a living Hollywood legend, let alone be his onscreen wife. Also starring on the show is Josh Duhamel. He plays Jimmy's protégé. Token chicks probably know Josh best from the years he spent on the long-running daytime soap, *All My Children*.

When I first met my "two Js," we immediately found our common thread. We're all golf maniacs.

Working on a television show sometimes means long fifteen-hour days. For actors those hours are usually spent the same way, acting, eating, and waiting to shoot a scene. I've got the acting part down and I love to eat, it's the waiting around that gets to all of us. But things are different on the set of *Las Vegas*. Since Jimmy and Josh both love to golf, we have practice nets behind the casino set on our show. The next time you're watching an episode and you see a shot of people playing slots, remember that on the other side of that wall, you can usually find Jimmy, Josh, or me whacking golf balls.

Jimmy is a blast to work and hang around with—he's a natural *wise guy*. The best example I can give you is the time I first met his mother.

We went to his trailer where she was waiting, and this is how Jimmy introduces me to his sweet mom: "Ma, this is Cheryl Ladd. Isn't she beautiful? I'm doin' her." WHAT! I was half laughing and half blushing. I shook her hand and said, almost nervously, "Only on the show."

She smirked and said, "Don't worry, I know, dear." She's obviously well accustomed to her son's humor. Born in the Bronx and raised in Queens, New York, Jimmy didn't see a lot of golf or tennis around the neighborhood. "I never even saw a golf club as a kid, and in my neighborhood a tennis racquet was something you used to strain spaghetti with. Golf wasn't something I had any interest in until about three or four years ago when I looked at my birth certificate and thought, it's time." At first he said he enjoyed playing just for the sake of being outside, hanging with friends, but when he started taking lessons, that hooked him completely.

"I have a great teacher, Greg Osborne, and the more lessons I took with him, the more I wanted to figure out why the ball goes this way, why it doesn't go that way, how do you make it do this and not that. It's a never-ending learning cycle, and I wanted to know all about it. What I need for golf is more hours in the day. I'll be playing, have a great swing thought that day, and I'm hitting the ball solid and good, and then I don't play for two or three weeks because of work and that just drives me friggin' nuts."

"Ahh, no, I was in my trailer reading Vogue."

One October night between scenes, Jimmy was in his trailer watching his beloved Yankees battle the Red Sox in the playoffs. In between innings I saw Jimmy standing outside his trailer working on his swing. I went to join him and maybe grab a few tips.

When I walked over the first thing he said was, "Did you see A-Rod's home run?"

"Ahh, no, I was in my trailer reading *Vogue*."

There used to be a popular commercial in the seventies that said, "When E.F. Hutton talks, people listen." We have a similar saying on the set of *Las Vegas*, "When Jimmy Caan talks, you better friggin' listen!" And his favorite subject to talk about is golf.

He's not a big fan of practicing. I bet a lot of you didn't know that in the seventies, Jimmy divided his time between being a movie star and a rodeo star. He'd work on a movie then leave town to join the traveling rodeo circuit. He was an excellent rider and even won some events. But a shoulder injury and the constant abuse to his body made him hang up his saddle. That's why he's not the biggest fan of practicing.

"Warming up before a round has never been my thing. Doing rodeo work really took a toll on my body, so in the morning when I wake up, I get out of bed in sections. I'll be on the golf course, and my hips will still be asleep in bed. That's why I only like to hit a few balls before I get out and play—any middle iron will do, like a seven or an eight—just to remember what it is I want to focus on with my golf swing that day."

So, Mr. Caan, tell us token chicks, exactly what is the focus in your swing?

"The main focal point for me is the finish. I don't think about the backswing, the downswing, nuthin'. Everything in golf happens from the ball forward. What I mean by that is nothing happens to the ball when you're in your backswing, it's just sitting there waiting for you to smack it. When I see golfers practicing at the range they're always checking their backswings. Am I in the right position here, am I good here, and more than likely, they have no idea what flaws they're even looking for. I think if you concentrate more on your finish position, you'll strike the ball better and with more consistency. Finding a good teacher is crucial. You need to be able to get along with each other and more importantly, speak the same language. That's why I like working with Greg. The first lesson I took with him, he said, 'Let me see your swing, I want to see how bad it is.' That's my kind of guy. He's got a lot of *you-know-what* to say that to me. I took a swing and the next thing he said was, 'Not bad, are you around a thirty handicap?' I almost popped him right there, but I was laughing too much."

I liked Jimmy's approach to ball striking. He was taking all the complexities out of it and focusing on one aspect, and you know what, it works great. I asked him to break it down for me.

Fig. 1

"Just because I'm focusing on the finish doesn't mean that everything else is taken for granted. Greg likes me to start the swing with a good foundation. He says to plant your right foot first and have it line up at a ninety-degree angle with your target (Fig. 1). Take hold of the club with your left hand first, and then complete your stance (Fig. 2, next page). The reason my teacher likes to start holding the club with the left hand first is to immediately get your shoulders in the same line as your target. When you grip the

He was taking all the complexities out of it and focusing on one aspect, and you know what, it works great. I asked him to break it down for me.

Fig. 2

Fig. 3

Fig. 4

club with the right hand first (Fig. 3), your right shoulder tends to point way right, giving you an excellent chance to hit a big ol' slice. When you take hold of the club with the left hand first, your left shoulder is in the same line as your clubface and your right foot, all pointing to your target (Fig. 4). This set-up allows it all to happen to the body naturally; nothing is forced. Now I'm set up completely square to the target. Greg says that most of his students are thinking of fifty million things when they step up to hit a golf ball, instead of one thought: the finish—the part of the swing that's going to direct the golf ball to the target with the proper distance, the way that a club was meant to be hit (Fig. 5).

"Now in order to get to that finish position properly you must lead the club with your hands. So your hands arrive at the ball a fraction of a second before the club makes contact (Figs. 6 and 7). This way, at impact you'll have no scooping action.

"A good thought to let this happen is to allow your left arm to extend completely during the follow-through. Try and maintain the straightness in your left arm, keeping it the same from when you set up to your backswing and through as you hit the

Fig. 5

Fig. 6

Fig. 7

ball. My swing thought for every shot is the same: 'finish to start.' Finish your swing to start the ball moving. By keeping your left arm constant through the swing, it gives you excellent extension and maximum hitting power."

Now about my other "J," Josh Duhamel. That night after I got the tips from Jimmy and he went to shoot his scene, I was passing along the newfound magic to Josh, when he said to me, "You know, I think my sister's a token chick too."

He told me a great story that had recently happened to his older sister, Ashlee. Growing up in North Dakota, Josh played a lot of golf and so did his sister. He said, "When we used to play together as teens I would look at her picture-perfect swing and just try to copy it." I'm sure that was also the goal for the men that Ashlee had her token chick moment with. Josh said that a few weeks back his sister was in Northern California watching a long-drive competition. This was a qualifying event for the big contest that was headed to none other than Las Vegas in the fall. (The city, not our show.)

Josh and I discussing golf ball technology. He's hardcore. I'm softcore.

"Ashlee wandered over to where the guys were warming up, starts talking golf with them, and the next thing she knows, one of them hands her a driver to hit a few. She takes the club and spanks one right down the middle, easily hitting it 250 yards. After that shot, without her even knowing it, one of the guys walked over and signed her up for the contest about to take place. She was sitting in the stands when all of a sudden her name was called to hit. She walked down from the stands, completely stunned, grabbed a club, and figured that everything happens for a reason, why not this? She hit the first three out of bounds, hits the next two pretty well, and then smacks her last drive 275 yards right down the pike. That drive qualified her for the finals in the ReMax World Long Drive Championship this fall in Las Vegas. So what do you think? Is she a token chick?"

I'll say she is. Way to go, Ashlee.

Now for you token chicks out there, here's a little info on Josh. He's single, gorgeous, and says, "Couples that play golf together have a one-up advantage on everyone else in sustaining their relationship. If you have that in common, it's the best four hours you can spend together." His mom has recently taken up the game and plays regularly with his dad, and they both love it.

Josh wanted me to pass along a tip from his sister that she's always telling him. "Shorten your backswing and don't try to hit it a mile. With a shorter backswing, you'll hit the ball purer and *will* hit it a mile without even having to try." I like that tip, especially coming from a long-drive qualifier.

Josh also had a tip of his own, "A few beers on the course can't hurt."

Now I have a tip for you, if you're a single woman, that is: find out whatever course Josh may be playing on, buy a six-pack, and tell him that you're a token chick. Then after your round with him, call me up so we can gossip.

TIPS FROM THE TOUR

In December 2003, I played in the pro-am at Tiger Woods' charity tournament, the Target World Challenge. It's an annual event held at the Sherwood Country Club in Thousand Oaks, California. Sherwood is amazing. Just ask some of the residents, like Wayne Gretzky and Kenny G: they're out there at the range every day, beating balls and getting ready for their next club championship. The Tiger Woods Foundation is as solid a charity as you'd expect from Tiger. His charities all share one main goal—making the lives of children better. His foundation offers everything from scholarships to sports programs for communities. The charity also sponsors a place called the St. Jude Children's Research Hospital, locat-

ed in Memphis. It's an amazing facility where children and their families stay while they receive treatment at the hospital. There's even a two hundred-seat covered outdoor arena where patients and their families can watch a movie or see a live concert.

Tiger is far and away the best role model out there. Period. With all his success and the commitments that make up his calendar, he still puts in a tremendous amount of time with his charities. Working with kids, giving golf clinics, visiting hospitals. This is the stuff you don't see him doing on television, but trust me, he's always out there *giving back*.

OK, back to the golf tournament. Of all the events I play in, this one is run the best. Everything is first-class, from the breakfast to the course to the amazing gift bag you get. (That's one of the best parts about any of these events. All token chicks love going to the makeup counter and getting the free bag. It's a vital part of any visit to the mall. The golf gift bag is no different. It's vital.) While I was at Sherwood that day I asked a few PGA pros and one sitcom star if they had any tips for us token chicks. Before I get to them I want to show you a visual tip directly from Tiger Woods. I was arriving at a par 3 on the back nine at Sherwood, and Tiger was on the green. You'll notice where he is in the picture in relation to where the pin is. Actually, first you'll notice what a breathtaking course Sherwood is.

Now why is Tiger walking from way in the back of the green to a pin that's located in the front? Did he miss the target by that much? Of course not. He was practicing where to hit his tee shot

Tiger practicing at Sherwood's beautiful par 3 sixteenth hole

for the pin placement he would face come Sunday. This was going to be a pivotal hole coming down the stretch, and Tiger was hitting shots to the usual Sunday pin placement—back and in the corner, the hardest part to reach on any green. This is a good tip for all of us who play regularly on the same course. When you're out there practicing, don't necessarily hit shots at the flag. Hit them to all areas of the green. Get to know how your home course greens break from different areas.

Before we get to the tips from the pros, here's a quick one of my own. When you're at the practice range, always stand next to a player who drives the ball well and lock those images into your head. You've heard of muscle memory—this is mental motivation memory. I like Billy Andrade's swing, and whenever I'm in a tournament with him I always watch his warm-up.

Now let's hear what some of my favorite pros have to say.

Mark O'Meara

I really like playing with women. They can be much better partners for golf than men. First off, they play quicker, and second, I'd rather look at a woman on the golf course than a man any day. In the pro-ams I play, we enjoy playing with a lady who loves the game and appreciates being out there. A lot of the time we get guys who can be grumpy about their game that day, and it's no fun for anyone. I find it's a nice change of pace when we have women compete in the tournaments, and I'd like to see more of it.

Tips for token chicks:

Usually for ladies the key issue is to try not to hit it so hard. When a woman tries to hit it farther, which is a normal tendency for all players, they tend to overswing and lose whatever power they do have. I would try a more compact swing and take a little bit more club. This will help you hit the ball solid.

For PGA pros playing with their wives:

I've always thought it would be quite interesting if we had a

I find it's a nice change of pace when we have women compete in the tournaments, and I'd like to see more of it.

tournament where tour players and their wives competed as teams against one another. I think they could really feel our pressure first-hand that way. Plus, it would be loads of fun.

Scott McCarron

My one tip for ladies is to work on the short game. Women golfers don't hit a lot of greens, and the better their short games are, the better they're going to score. Most amateurs in general just work on hitting the driver and trying to hit it as far as they can. When we're practicing, we spend 80 percent of our time on the short game.

Duffy Waldorf

Women players focus a little too much on their long game. Male players suffer from that problem too. Men and women both need to put time into their short games. Really the first lesson in golf is learning to hit the ball solid and worrying about everything else after. The best way to learn how to make solid contact is by practicing your short game.

As far as men playing golf with their wives goes, I think it's a great idea for couples to play together. Especially after you've just returned from church. That way you've gotten everything in perspective, and it'll keep you from cursing out there on Sunday afternoon.

The best way to learn how to make solid contact is by practicing your short game.

Jay Hass

I think everybody overlooks the play around the greens. I've played in mixed team events with LPGA players for fifteen years. I was actually a little surprised to see that many of them weren't as sharp around the greens as I was expecting. I think most golfers, professionals included, are too consumed with doing it right technically, and they forget how important the play around the greens is. Even the best players miss five or six greens a round on an average. If you don't have a short game, you're just giving away a bunch of strokes. It's amazing that when a person has a bad round and shoots a poor score, they immediately come out to the driving range and work on the wrong thing. They try to fix that one bad iron shot that they think ruined their round. You need savvy around the greens. I don't think there's any secret to hitting a golf ball. There's an old expression: "It's in the dirt." Just beat a bunch of balls, and you'll figure it out.

But I think that all players need to figure out a system when it comes to their short game. From practice to execution. Figure out what short-game shots you're good at and put them into play.

Kevin James

It's nice to play in a tournament with Cheryl. We're usually the only two women that are in these golf events. Just kidding, although I wish they would let me hit from the ladies' tees. My fiancée has just taken up the game, and she loves it. She can really hit the ball. She encourages me to play as much as I want when I'm not working. My buddies are telling me that she's setting me up by making me think she doesn't mind, that it's all part of the engagement process, that once we get married, it's all going to change, it'll be over. No more golf. And once we have kids, it will be totally over. I won't even be allowed to watch golf on television.

As far as playing golf with women goes, I've learned that they play a lot smarter than I do. Their shot selection is always better and more thought out than mine. They're not going to hit it as far as men do, so they know their limits and work that logic into what shots they choose to hit. That's having good course management. I guess it's also why in most families, it's usually the mom who runs the show. She's the only one who could coordinate three meals for everyone a day, clean the house, get kids off to school, and sometimes even work a full-time job! That's why course management comes so naturally to them and it comes so hard to us guys. We can't even clean out the garage when they ask.

This seems to be a request from every pro-am partner I'm paired with.

But I know how to get even . . .

A hot dog loaded with mustard and onions does the trick!

Now this is how you freshen up after a round! Check out this ladies' locker room. That's correct, you read me right. This is the ladies' locker room at Sherwood. Pretty fancy-shmancy I'd say. It's the perfect setting for any token chick to end her round. Ta Ta.